SEVEN NIGHTS

Jorge Luis Borges

SEVEN NIGHTS

translated by Eliot Weinberger
introduction by Alastair Reid

faber and faber

LONDON · BOSTON

First published in Mexico in 1980 as *Siete Noches*
by Fondo de Cultura Económica
First published in the USA in 1984
by New Directions Publishing Corporation, New York
and simultaneously in Canada
by George G. McLeod Limited, Toronto
First published in Great Britain in 1986
by Faber and Faber Limited
3 Queen Square London WC1N 3AU

Printed in Great Britain by
Redwood Burn Ltd, Trowbridge, Wiltshire
All rights reserved

© Fondo de Cultura Económica 1980
translation © Eliot Weinberger 1984
introduction © Alastair Reid 1984

'The Thousand and One Nights' first appeared
in translation in *The Georgia Review*
'Blindness' first appeared in translation in
Harper's Magazine

British Library Cataloguing in Publication Data

Borges, Jorge Luis
Seven nights.
I. Title   II. Siete noches. *English*
086′.1   PQ7797.B635

ISBN 0–571–13737–7

Contents

Introduction

THE SEVEN LECTURES which make up this volume were delivered by Borges in Buenos Aires at the Teatro Coliseo, at intervals between June and August 1977. In an Epilogue to the first Spanish edition of the book, published in Mexico in 1980, Roy Bartholomew tells how the lectures were widely taped, appeared later as pirated records, and were printed, in a cut and mangled form, in the literary supplement of a Buenos Aires newspaper. Later, at a remove of two years, he worked on a version of the lectures with Borges, who corrected them extensively for publication.

Among his many other literary selves, Borges has had a separate existence as a lecturer for almost the past forty years, and, like every separate dimension of Borges, the lectures shed a different kind of light on the whole, and make clear more of Borges' webbed connections. Borges' dismissal from his post in the suburban library in 1946 had made lecturing his essential means of earning a livelihood, but he undertook it with some trepidation for, unable to read a written text, he had first to prepare the lectures, with his mother's help, and then commit them to memory. Yet the obligation to memorize his material did Borges a great service, for, as his blindness encroached, he was at the same time memorizing a considerable private library of reference and quotation. Asked a question now, he will pause, as though riffling through bookshelves in his head, and come up with a verse from one of his essential texts, an idiosyncratic collection familiar to his readers. Certain lectures, like Borges' endlessly shifting lecture on Dante, which he has given many times, but probably never twice in the same form, exist by now in that remembered library, and it is appropriate that this group of them become part of the Borges canon.

From the seventies on, however, Borges has traveled, lectured, and granted interviews with relative abandon, throughout Europe, South America, and the United States, and there his past lecturing experience has served him well, for it has meant that he has had ready an eclectic range of succinct literary opinions and an abundance of quotation, and has given memorable interviews. Borges' presence is an intensely moving one, and since, in the last ten years especially, he has been seen on television by vast numbers of people, his presence has become fastened to his written image, so that at certain times he appears to be a pure embodiment of his own writing. He prefers of late to give *charlas* rather than formal lectures, but then, whatever Borges is talking about, it is his manner to make sudden shifts and connections as they occur to him, so that the lecture becomes a series of separate insights linked by the eccentric thread of Borges' attention. Of his indefatigable traveling, he remaked to me last year: "In Buenos Aires, one day is much like another . . . But when I travel, I move from one comfortable armchair to another, a kindly ghost materializes and talks to me, very informedly, about my writings, then vanishes, to be replaced at once with another. It makes for great variety."

I have listened and talked to Borges over the last twenty years in a variety of speaking contexts—in London, Oxford,

Scotland, Spain, Buenos Aires, and New York—and have come to admire the range and fascinations of the spoken Borges, as distinct from the written one. The terse and scrupulous texts of the written Borges we all know well— their spare inevitability, their disquieting, sometimes dizzying effect, their singular vocabulary, of images as well as words. Some words have become his—one could not use the word *vertiginoso* without being intensely aware of him, for his work defines it. We know from his essays the play of his mind, his speculative ironies, his obliqueness, the surprising connections he makes; and, through his poems, we come to know his obsessions, and his essential metaphors.

The spoken Borges, however, is much more elusive, and Protean. Where his writings show language as a game, his conversation quite often becomes play, a demonstration of ironies. He will quite often be deliberately perverse, making an apparently outrageous statement, and arguing it toward sense. "All literature is really for children," he will say suddenly, and then he will go on to make a brilliant case. Borges' conversational speculations follow a thread of his own, and his wiser interviewers have let his mind move of its own accord, content to keep track. Something may give him a reason to quote Oscar Wilde, and he will go on to talk about Wilde, about the French language, his schooldays in Geneva, Calvin, the Scots, always turning to the library in his memory. Everything connects, but it is Borges alone who can make these connections, across cultures, across literatures, across languages, across time.

The lectures in this book all reveal these connected shifts in Borges' attention, the flow of his mind and memory. In understanding Borges, it is important to remember that, for him, literary experience has been more vivid and affecting than real experience, or, better said, that there is no sensible difference between the two; so that when Borges is talking about books and writers, it is like talking of land-scapes and journeys, so vivid has his reading been to him. Through literature, he maintains, we can travel through time, and become all men; it is his Aleph. So, his lectures wander along the thread of a preoccupation, as in the lecture on "Nightmares," and shift from personal memories to writers, to an examination of other people's metaphors, to language itself. There is nothing formal about Borges' literary speculations. Criticism, he has reminded us, is simply a branch of imaginative literature; and, while the play of his mind makes material for critics, Borges is not much concerned with literary judgment. For him, literature at its highest point generates awe, the disquieting astonish-ment that arises from a poem, a deep image, a crucial paragraph, what he calls either *asombro* or *sagrada horror*, "holy dread." The writers he reaches for are those who have given him this essential experience; and it is what most distinguishes his own work, when, in a few phrases, the sharp edges of reality quiver in doubt, the awe is tangible. The lectures are separate literary journeys that we could not take by ourselves. Borges is our Virgil; only he knows the way.

The presence of Borges sometimes takes on an un-canny dimension: at certain times, he seems to be living his own metaphors. If he is asked about some remark he made years ago, he is likely to disclaim it, saying that it was obviously made by Borges, the Other. The figure of the other Borges, the writer, to whom the living Borges is chained, is familiar to us from poems and prose pieces, but in conversation, he dramatizes the division, and makes us feel it directly. His work generates its own awe, but his presence intensifies it: those who have heard him are after-ward better able to catch the wavelength of his writing, hearing that frail, precise voice threading its way through the words.

It is important, then, in reading these lectures, to imagine them spoken by Borges, and to follow the shifts in his text as if they were the shifts in a living attention, for the lectures also demonstrate the difference between the spoken and the written: the language has not been tempered down to written inevitability. There is a speaker present, the thread of a voice to follow. One has only to imagine the lecture on "Blindness" being delivered by a blind Borges to realize that his presence added a moving dimension to the language of the lecture.

It is just and appropriate that Borges' lectures should appear in an English version, since he has delivered many similar lectures in English. Borges speaks English with great respect and a careful formality. Since his early days in his father's English library, he has always thought of English as the language of literature, Spanish the language of real life, and his English does have certain mannerisms that come more from literature than from the spoken reality. Eliot Weinberger's translation has been careful to keep Borges' precise phrasing and tone. His version sounds like Borges in English. Wisely, since the original Spanish text was a corrected transcript, he has made essential alterations in the text, removing certain repetitions, to give the spoken sentences a written fluency. Paradoxically, while Borges' written texts are as spare as any great writer's, he has been generous with himself in the form of lectures and interviews. These lectures, in this able version, save something from that prodigal flow.

ALASTAIR REID

The Divine Comedy

PAUL CLAUDEL HAS WRITTEN—in a page unworthy of Paul Claudel—that the spectacles awaiting us after death will no doubt little resemble those that Dante showed us in the *Inferno*, the *Purgatorio*, and the *Paradiso*.

This curious remark is a proof of the intensity of Dante's text: the fact that while reading the poem, or remembering it later, we tend to believe that Dante imagined the other world exactly as he presented it. We inevitably assume that Dante believed that after death he would encounter the inverted mountain of Hell or the terraces of Purgatory or the concentric heavens of Paradise. Moreover, he would speak with shades—shades of classical Antiquity—and some of them would reply in Italian tercets.

This is, of course, absurd. Claudel's observation corresponds not to reason—for to rationalize it is to realize it's absurd—but rather to a sentiment, and one which could isolate us from the pleasure, the intense pleasure, of reading the work.

There is a great deal of evidence that refutes this. One is a statement attributed to Dante's son. He said that his father had proposed to show the life of sinners through the image of Hell, the life of penitents through the image of Purgatory, and the life of the just through the image of Paradise. He did not read it in a literal way. We have, moreover, Dante's own testimony, in the epistle to the Can Grande della Scala.

The epistle has been considered apocryphal, but it could not have been written much later than Dante. Whoever wrote it, it is believable as a product of its time. In it, the author affirms that the *Commedia* may be read four ways: literal, moral, anagogical, and allegorical. Dante, then, would be the symbol of man, Beatrice of faith, and Virgil of reason.

The idea of a text capable of multiple readings is characteristic of the Middle Ages, those maligned and complex Middle Ages that gave us Gothic architecture, the Icelandic sagas, and the Scholastic philosophy in which everything was discussed. That gave us, above all, the *Commedia*, which we continue to read, and which continues to astonish us; which will last beyond our lives, far beyond our waking lives, and will be enriched by each generation of readers.

Dante never presumed that what he was showing us corresponded to a real image of the world of death. Nothing of the kind. Dante could not possibly have thought that.

I believe, nevertheless, in the usefulness of that ingenious concept: the idea that what we are reading is a true story. It serves to carry us away. Personally, I am a hedonistic reader; I have never read a book merely because it was ancient. I read books for the aesthetic emotions they offer me, and I ignore the commentaries and criticism. When I first read the *Commedia*, I was carried away. I read it as I had read other, less famous works. I would like to tell you—since we are among friends, and since I am talking not to all of you, but rather with each one of you—the story of my personal involvement with the *Commedia*.

It all began shortly before the dictatorship. I was employed in a library in the Almagro section of Buenos Aires. I lived at Las Heras and Pueyrredón, and I had to travel by slow and solitary streetcars all the way from the north side of town to Almagro South, to the library at Avenida La Plata and Carlos Calvo. Chance—except that there is no chance; what we call chance is our ignorance of the complex machinery of causality—led me to discover three small volumes in the Mitchell Bookstore (now gone—it brings back many memories). Those three volumes—I should have brought one with me, as a talisman—were the *Inferno*, the *Purgatorio*, and the *Paradiso*, in the English version by Carlyle (not Thomas Carlyle). They were very handy books, published by Dent. They fit into my pocket. On the left was the Italian text, and on the right a literal translation. I devised this modus operandi: I first read a verse, a tercet, in the English prose; then I read the verse in Italian; and so on through to the end of the canto. Then I read the whole canto in English, and finally in Italian. With that first reading I realized that the translations were no substitute for the original text. The translation could be, at best, a means and a stimulus for the reader to approach the original. This was especially true for a Spanish reader. I think that Cervantes, somewhere in *Don Quixote*, says that with two cents of the Tuscan language one can understand Ariosto.

Well, those two cents were given to me by the semantic brotherhood of Spanish and Italian. I observed at the time that poetry, above all the great poetry of Dante, is much more than what it says. Poetry is, among so many other things, an intonation, an accentuation that is often untranslatable. I saw this from the beginning. When I reached the peak of Paradise, when I reached the deserted Paradise, there, at that moment in which Dante is abandoned by

Virgil and he finds himself alone and calls out to him, at that moment I felt I could read the Italian text directly, only occasionally looking at the English. So I read the three volumes on those slow streetcar rides. Later I read other editions.

I have read the *Commedia* many times. The truth is that I don't know Italian. I only know the Italian Dante taught me, and later Ariosto, when I read *Orlando Furioso*. And then the simpler parts of Croce. I have read almost all of Croce, and though I am not always in agreement with him, I am enchanted by him. Enchantment, as Stevenson said, is one of the special qualities a writer must have. Without enchantment, the rest is useless.

I have read the *Commedia* many times, in all of the editions I could find, and I have been distracted by the different commentaries, the varied interpretations of that multifaceted work. (Of all the editions, three in particular are noteworthy: those by Attilio Momigliano, Carlo Grabher, and Hugo Steiner.) I have found that in the oldest editions theological commentary predominates; in the nineteenth century, historical; and currently, aesthetic, which directs us toward the accentuation of each line, one of the great virtues of Dante.

I have compared Dante to Milton, but Milton has only one music: what they call in English a "sublime style." That music is always the same, regardless of the emotions of the characters. In Dante, however, as in Shakespeare, the music corresponds to the emotions. Intonation and accentuation are foremost; each phrase must be read aloud.

Truly fine poetry must be read aloud. A good poem does not allow itself to be read in a low voice or silently. If we can read it silently, it is not a valid poem: a poem demands pronunciation. Poetry always remembers that it was an oral art before it was a written art. It remembers that it was first song.

There are two lines which confirm this. One is in Homer —or the Greeks whom we call Homer—where he says, in the *Odyssey,* "The gods weave misfortunes for men, so that the generations to come will have something to sing about." The other, much later, is from Mallarmé, who repeats, less beautifully, what Homer said: "*tout aboutit en un livre,*" everything ends up in a book. The Greeks speak of generations that will sing; Mallarmé speaks of an object, of a thing among things, a book. But the idea is the same: the idea that we are made for art, we are made for memory, we are made for poetry, or perhaps we are made for oblivion. But something remains, and that something is history or poetry, which are not essentially different.

Carlyle and other critics have observed that the most notable characteristic of Dante is intensity. If we think of the hundred cantos of the poem, it seems a miracle that that intensity never lets up, except in a few places in the *Paradiso* which for the poet were light and for us are shadow. I can't think of another example, except perhaps *Macbeth*, which begins with the three witches and continues to the death of the hero without a weak moment.

I would like to mention another aspect: the gentleness of Dante. We always think of the somber and sententious Florentine poem, and we forget that the work is full of delights, of pleasures, of tenderness. That tenderness is part of the structure of the work. For example, Dante must have read somewhere that the cube is the most solid of volumes. It was a current, unpoetical observation, and yet Dante used it as a metaphor for man, who must support misfortune: "*buon tetragono a i colpe di fortuna,*" man is a good tetragon, a cube. That is truly rare.

I'd also like to recall the curious metaphor of the arrow.

Dante wants to make us feel the speed of the arrow as it leaves the bow and hits the target. He tells us that it is fixed in the target, that it shoots from the bow, and leaves the string. He inverts the beginning and end to show how quickly this has occurred.

There is a verse that is always in my memory. It is the one in the first canto of the *Purgatorio* where he refers to that morning, that incredible morning on the mountain of Purgatory, at the South Pole. Dante, who has left the filth, the sadness, and the horror of Hell, says, "*dolce color d'oriental zaffiro*." The lines impose that slowness on the voice:

> *dolce color d'oriental zaffiro*
> *che s'accoglieva nel sereno aspetto*
> *del mezzo puro infino al primo giro.*

I would like to linger over the curious mechanism of this verse—but the word *mechanism* is too harsh for what I want to say. Dante describes the Eastern sky, describes the dawn, and compares the color of the dawn to a sapphire. He compares it to a sapphire called *Oriental sapphire*, a sapphire of the East. The line is a game of mirrors, since the Orient is the color of the sapphire and the sapphire is an Oriental sapphire. That is to say, the sapphire is weighted with the riches of the word *Oriental*. It is full of *The Thousand and One Nights*, which Dante did not know, but which nevertheless is there.

I will also recall the famous last line of the fifth canto of the *Inferno:* "*e caddi come corpo morto cade.*" The fall resounds through the repetition of the word *fall*.

The *Commedia* is full of felicities of this kind. But what sustains the poem is that it is a narrative. When I was young, narrative was scorned. It was considered to be nothing more than anecdote. It was forgotten that poetry began by being narrative, that the roots of poetry are the epic, that the epic is the first poetic genre. In the epic there is time: a before, during, and after. All of that is in poetry.

I would advise the reader to ignore the feud between the Guelphs and Ghibellines, Scholastic philosophy, the mythological allusions, and the lines of Virgil which Dante repeats, sometimes improving them, as excellent as they are in the original Latin. It is better, at least in the beginning, merely to follow the story. I don't think anyone can keep from doing so.

We enter, then, into a story, and we enter in a way that is almost magical. Normally, when dealing with the super-natural, one has an unbelieving writer guiding unbelieving readers, and he must prepare them for what is to come. Dante does not need this: "*Nel mezzo del cammin di nostra vita/mi rotrovai per una selva oscura.*" That is, at thirty-five I found myself in a dark forest. It may be allegorical, but we physically believe it. Thirty-five is halfway through life because the Bible prescribes a life of seventy years for the prudent man. It is assumed that everything after seventy is *bleak*, as the English say; everything is sadness and anxiety. So when Dante writes, "*nel mezzo del cammin di nostra vita,*" he is not exercising a vague rhetoric. He is telling us exactly the date of his vision.

I don't think that Dante was a visionary. A vision is brief. A vision as large as the *Commedia* is impossible. His vision was voluntary: we may abandon ourselves to it and read it with poetic faith. Coleridge said that poetic faith is the willing suspension of disbelief. If we attend the theater, we know that, amid the scenery, there are costumed people speaking the words of Shakespeare or Ibsen or Pirandello which have been put in their mouths. But we accept that these people are not costumed, that the man in the antechamber slowly talking to himself of vengeance really is Hamlet, Prince of Denmark. We lose ourselves. Films are even stranger, for what we are seeing are not disguised people but photographs of disguised people, and yet we believe them while the film is being shown.

In the case of Dante, everything is so vivid that we begin to imagine that he believed in his other world, in the same way that he believed in a geocentric astronomy and not in other astronomies.

We believe Dante so profoundly for a reason that was pointed out by Paul Groussac: because the *Commedia* is written in the first person. It is not a mere grammatical artifice; it does not mean saying *I saw* for *they saw* or *it was*. It means something more. It means that Dante is one of the characters of the *Commedia*. According to Groussac, this was a new development. Before Dante, St. Augustine had written his *Confessions*. But those confessions, because of their splendid rhetoric, are not as close to us as Dante is; the rhetoric interposes itself between what he wants to say and what we hear.

Rhetoric must be a bridge, a road; too often it is a wall, an obstacle. We see it in writers as diverse as Seneca, Quevedo, Milton, and Lugones. In all of them the words come between them and us.

We know Dante more intimately than his contemporaries. One might say that we know him as he knew Virgil, who was a dream of his. We certainly know him better than we know Beatrice Portinari, better than anyone. He has placed himself in the center of the action. Everything is not only seen by him, but he is also an active participant. But his role is not always in accord with what he is describing.

We see Dante terrified by Hell. He must be terrified, not because he is a coward but rather so that we will believe in Hell. Dante is terrified, he is afraid, he comments on this and that. We know his opinions not by what he says but by the poetics, the intonation, the accentuation of his language.

There is another character. (In fact, there are three, but I will now speak of the second.) And that is Virgil. Dante has succeeded in giving us a second image of Virgil. The first is the image left us by the *Aeneid* or the *Georgics*. The second, the more intimate image, has been given to us by poetry, by Dante's pious poetry.

One of the subjects of literature—as it is of life—is friendship. I would say that friendship is the Argentine passion. There are many friendships in literature, which is a web of friendship: Quixote and Sancho; Fierro and Cruz, our two gauchos lost in the frontier; the old soldier and Fabio Cáceres; Kim and the lama. Friendship is a common theme, but in general writers tend to emphasize the contrast between the two friends.

In the case of Dante, the matter is more delicate. It is not exactly a contrast, although there is a filial relationship. Dante comes to be the son of Virgil, yet at the same time he is superior to Virgil for he believes he will be saved, since he has been given the vision. But he knows, from the beginning, that Virgil is a lost soul, a reprobate. When Virgil tells him that he cannot accompany him beyond Purgatory, he knows that the Latin poet will always inhabit the terrible *nobile castello* with the great shades of Antiquity, those who never heard the word of Christ. At that moment, Dante hails him with magnificent words: "*Tu, duca; tu, signore; tu, maestro* . . ." He speaks of the great labor and of the great love with which his work has been studied, and this relation is always maintained between the two. But Virgil is essentially a sad figure who knows he is forever condemned to that castle filled with the absence of God. Dante, however, will be permitted to see God; he will be permitted to understand the universe.

We have, first, two characters. And then there are the thousands, hundreds, a multitude of characters of whom it has been said that they are episodic. I would call them eternal.

A contemporary novel requires five or six hundred pages to make us know somebody, if it ever does. For Dante a single moment is enough. In that moment a person is defined forever. Dante unconsciously sought that central moment. I have wanted to do the same in many stories, and I have been admired for a discovery which actually belongs to Dante in the Middle Ages: that of presenting a moment as a cipher of a life. In Dante we have characters whose lives may consist of only a few tercets, and yet their lives are eternal. They live in a word, in a gesture; they need do nothing more. They are merely part of a canto, but that part is eternal. They keep living and renewing themselves in the memory and in the imagination of men.

Carlyle said that there are two characteristics of Dante. Of course there are others, but two are essential: tenderness and rigor, which do not contradict one another. On the one hand, there is his human tenderness, what Shakespeare called "the milk of human kindness." On the other, there is the knowledge that we are inhabitants of a rigorous world, that there is an order to it. That order corresponds to the Other, the third speaker.

Let us recall two examples. First, the best-known episode of the *Inferno*, the story of Paolo and Francesca in the fifth canto. I would not presume to summarize what Dante has said—it would be irreverent for me to say in other words what Dante has said for always in his Italian—but I'd like simply to recall the circumstances.

Dante and Virgil arrive at the second circle. There they see the whirlwind of souls and smell the stench of sin, the stench of punishment. There is Minos, twining his tail around himself to indicate to which circle the condemned must descend. It is physically disagreeable, deliberately ugly, because it is understood that in Hell nothing can be beautiful.

In that circle where the lustful are punished there are great, illustrious names. I say "great names" because Dante, when he began the canto, had not yet reached the perfection of his art, the point where the characters became something more than their names. But halfway through the canto, Dante makes his great discovery: the possibility of a dialogue between the souls of the dead and Dante himself, who will respond and judge in his fashion. No, he will not judge them. He knows that he is not the Judge, that the Judge is the Other, the third speaker, the Divinity.

Well then: there are Helen, Achilles, Paris, Tristan, and other luminaries. But Dante sees two whom he does not know, less illustrious, and who belong to the contemporary world: Paolo and Francesca. He knows that they have both died as adulterers. He calls to them and they come, "*quali colombe dal disio chiamate.*" Here we have two sinners, and Dante compares them to two doves called by desire, because sensuality must also be the essence of the scene. They draw near, and Francesca, who is the only one to speak—Paolo cannot—thanks him for calling them and speaks these pathetic words: "*Se fosse amico il Re dell'universo/ noi pregheremmo lui per la tua pace,*" if we were friends of the King of the universe—she cannot say God, because that name is forbidden in Hell and Purgatory —we would pray for your peace, since you have taken pity on our misfortune.

Francesca tells her story, and she tells it twice. The first time she tells it in a reserved fashion, but she insists that she is still in love with Paolo. Repentence is forbidden in Hell. She knows she has sinned and must continue to be faithful to her sin, which gives her a heroic grandeur. It would be terrible if she repented, if she denied what happened. Francesca knows the punishment is just; she accepts it, and continues to love Paolo.

Dante is curious about one thing. "*Amor condusse noi ad una morte*": Paolo and Francesca were executed together. Dante is not interested in adultery, nor in the way they were discovered and brought to justice. What interests him is something more intimate, and that is how they knew they were in love, how they fell in love, how they reached the time of the sweet sighs. He asks them.

To digress for a moment, I would like to recall a stanza, perhaps the finest, of Leopoldo Lugones, who was no doubt inspired by the fifth canto of the *Inferno*. It is the first quatrain of his "*Alma venturosa*" ("Fortunate soul"), one of the sonnets of *Las horas doradas* ("*The golden hours*") of 1922:

> *Al promediar la tarde de aquel día,*
> *Cuando iba mi habitual adiós a darte,*
> *Fue una vaga congoja de dejarte*
> *Lo que me hizo saber que te quería.*

[Halfway through the afternoon that day,| As I bid you my habitual goodbye,| A vague dismay at leaving| Made me know that I loved you.]

An inferior poet would have said that a man feels great sadness on leaving his woman, and he would have said that they see each other rarely. In contrast, "As I bid you my habitual goodbye" may be a slow and heavy line, but it expresses that they see each other frequently. And then: "A vague dismay at leaving/ Made me know that I loved you."

The theme is essentially the same in the fifth canto: two people who discover that they are in love and didn't know it. This is what Dante wants to know; he wants them to tell him how it happened. She tells how, to entertain themselves one day, they were reading about Lancelot and how he complained of love. They were alone and suspected nothing. They did not suspect they were in love. And they were reading a story from the *Matière de Bretagne*, one of those books conceived by the British in France after the Saxon invasion—one of those books that fed the madness of Alonso Quijano and revealed their guilty love to Paolo and Francesca. Well: Francesca states that at times they blushed. Then, "*quando leggemmo il disiato riso*," when we read how the longed-for smile was kissed by such a lover, this one, who will never be separated from me, kissed my mouth, *tutto tremante*.

There is something that Dante does not say, but which one feels at a distance from the episode and perhaps gives it its virtue. Dante relates the fate of the two lovers with an infinite pity, and we sense that he envies their fate. Paolo and Francesca are in Hell and he will be saved, but they have loved and he never won the love of the woman he loved, Beatrice. There is a certain injustice to this, and Dante must feel it as something terrible, now that he is separated from her. In contrast, these two sinners are together. They cannot speak to each other, they turn in the black whirlwind without hope, yet they are together. When she speaks, she says "we," speaking for the two of them, another form of being together. They are together for eternity; they share Hell—and that, for Dante, must have been a kind of Paradise.

We know that he is quite moved. He then collapses as though he were dead.

Everyone is defined forever in a single instant of their lives, a moment in which a man encounters his self for always. It has been said that Dante is cruel toward Francesca, by condemning her. But that is to ignore the Third Character. The judgment of God does not always coincide with the feelings of Dante. Those who do not understand the *Commedia* say that Dante wrote it to take revenge on his enemies and to reward his friends. There is nothing more false. Nietzsche said, slanderously, that Dante is a hyena making verses among the tombs. A versifying hyena is a contradiction; moreover, Dante does not enjoy suffering. He knows that there are unpardonable, capital sins. For each he selects a person who has committed that sin. But in each there may be something admirable or worthy. Francesca and Paolo are not merely voluptuaries. They have committed no other sin, but one is enough to condemn them.

The idea of God as indecipherable is a concept we find in another of the essential books of mankind, the *Book of Job*. You will recall how Job condemns God, how his friends defend Him, and how at the end God speaks from the whirlwind and rebukes equally those who accuse or defend Him. God is beyond all human justice, as He Himself declares in the *Book of Job*. And the men humble themselves before God, because they have dared to judge Him, to defend Him. It is unnecessary. God, as Nietzsche would say, is beyond good and evil. He is another category.

If Dante had always agreed with the God he imagines, it would have meant that his was a false god, merely a replica of Dante himself. However, Dante must accept his God, as he must accept that Beatrice never loved him, that

Florence is vile, as he will have to accept his exile and his death in Ravenna. He must accept the evil of the world, and at the same time, he must worship a God he does not understand.

There is a character missing in the *Commedia*, one who could not be there because he had become too human. That character is Jesus. He does not appear in the *Commedia* as he appears in the Gospels; the human Jesus of the Gospels could not be the Second Person of the Trinity that the *Commedia* requires.

I would like to turn to the second example, which for me is the high point of the *Commedia*. It occurs in the twenty-sixth canto, and it is the episode of Ulysses. (I once wrote an article titled "The Enigma of Ulysses." I published it, but later lost it, and I'd like to try to reconstruct it now.) I think that it is the most enigmatic of the episodes of the *Commedia*, and perhaps the most intense. But it is very difficult, when dealing with peaks, to know which is the highest—and the *Commedia* is made of peaks.

I have chosen the *Commedia* for this first talk because I am a man of letters and I believe that the apex of literature, of all literature, is the *Commedia*. This does not imply that I agree with its theology, or with its mythology, which is a combination of Christian and pagan myth. What it means is that no book has given me such intense aesthetic emotions. And, I repeat, I am a hedonistic reader; I look for emotion in books.

The *Commedia* is a book that everyone ought to read. Not to do so is to deprive oneself of the greatest gift that literature can give us; it is to submit to a strange asceticism. Why should we deny ourselves the joy of reading the *Commedia*? Besides, it is not difficult to read. What is difficult is outside of the reading: the opinions, the discussions. But the book itself is crystalline. And there is the central character, Dante, who is perhaps the most vivid character in literature, not to mention the other characters. But I will return to the episode of Ulysses.

They reach a ditch, I think it is the eighth, the one of swindlers. There is, in the beginning, an apostrophe against Florence, where he says that it beats its wings over heaven and earth and its name is spread through Hell. Then he sees above him countless flames, and inside the flames are the dark souls of the swindlers, dark because they continue to hide themselves. The flames move, and Dante almost falls. Virgil holds him back—the words of Virgil. He speaks of those who are inside the flames, and Virgil mentions two great names, Ulysses and Diomedes. They are there because together they plotted the strategy of the Trojan horse, which allowed the Greeks to enter the besieged city.

There are Ulysses and Diomedes, and Dante wants to meet them. He tells Virgil his desire to speak with these illustrious ancient shades, these celebrated and great ancient heroes. Virgil approves, but asks him to leave the talking to him, since we are dealing with two proud Greeks—it is better if Dante does not speak. This has been explained in various ways. Torquato Tasso believed that Virgil wanted to surpass Homer. That suspicion is totally absurd, for Virgil sang of Ulysses and Diomedes, and if Dante knows them it was because Virgil made them known. We may ignore the hypothesis that Dante was scorned because he was a descendant of Aeneas, a barbarian, worthless to the Greeks. Virgil, like Diomedes and Ulysses, is a dream of Dante's. Dante is dreaming them, but he dreams them with such intensity, in a way that is so vivid, that he can believe that those dreams—which have no other voice than that which he gives them, no other form than that which he lends them—may scorn him, he who is nobody, who hasn't even written his *Commedia*.

Dante has entered the game, as we enter it: Dante too is swindled by the *Commedia*. He thinks: they are celebrated heroes of Antiquity, and I am nobody, a poor man. Why should they take notice of what I say to them? Then Virgil asks them to tell how they died, and the voice of the invisible Ulysses speaks. Ulysses has no face; he is within the flame.

Here we come to what is wonderful, a legend created by Dante, a legend superior to many in the *Odyssey* or the *Aeneid*, or those that will be included in that other book in which Ulysses appears, as Sinbad of the Sea (Sinbad the Sailor), *The Thousand and One Nights*.

The legend was suggested to Dante by various things; above all, the belief that the city of Lisbon was founded by Ulysses and the stories of the Fortunate Isles in the Atlantic. The Celts were thought to have populated the Atlantic coast from those fantastic lands: an island with a river that rises up and crosses the sky and is full of boats and fish that do not fall back to earth; a revolving island of fire; an island where bronze greyhounds chase silver deer. Some of this must have been known to Dante; what is important is what he made of these legends. He originated something that is essentially noble.

Ulysses leaves Penelope. He calls together his companions and reminds them that, although they are now old and married men, they have crossed thousands of dangers with him. He proposes a noble enterprise: to pass through the Pillars of Hercules and cross the sea, to explore the Southern Hemisphere, which, it was then believed, was a hemisphere of water—it was not known if anyone was there. He tells them that they are men, not beasts; they have been born for courage, for knowledge; they have been born to know and to understand.

They follow him and "make wings of their oars." (It is curious that this metaphor is also found in the *Odyssey*, which Dante could not have known.) They sail and leave behind Ceuta and Seville, enter the open sea, and turn toward the left. (Toward the left, or on the left, means evil in the *Commedia*. To climb to Purgatory one goes to the right; to descend to Hell, to the left. That is to say, the "sinister" side has a double meaning.) Then he tells us, "in the night I saw all the stars of the other hemisphere"—our hemisphere, the Southern, full of stars. (The great Irish poet Yeats speaks of the "starladen sky." That is untrue in the Northern Hemisphere, where there are few stars compared to ours.)

They sail for five months and then, at last, see land. What they see is a brown mountain in the distance, a mountain taller than any they have ever seen. Ulysses says that their joy was soon turned to grief, for a whirlwind blew from the land and the ship was lost. That mountain is Purgatory, as we will learn in another canto. Dante believes that Purgatory—he pretends to believe in poetic justice—is antipodal to the city of Jerusalem.

Well, we reach that terrible moment, and we wonder why Ulysses has been punished. Evidently it was not for the ruse of the Trojan horse, since the culminating moment of his life, the one told to Dante and to us, is another: it is that generous, bold enterprise of wanting to know the forbidden, the impossible. We ask ourselves why this canto has such force. Before answering I would like to mention something which has never been said before, as far as I know.

It is that other great book, a great poem of our times, *Moby-Dick* by Herman Melville, who certainly knew Dante in the Longfellow translation. We have the mad enterprise of the crippled Captain Ahab, who wants to revenge himself on the white whale. At the end they find the whale, who sinks the ship, and the great novel ends exactly as Dante's canto ends: the sea closes over them. Melville must have remembered the *Commedia* at that point, though I prefer to think that he had read it and absorbed it in such a way he could literally forget it; that the *Commedia* had become part of him, and that he could rediscover what he had read years before. But the story is the same, except that Ahab is not moved by a noble aim but rather by a desire for vengeance. Ulysses, in contrast, acts as the greatest of men. Moreover, he invokes a just reason, one related to intelligence, and he is punished.

To what do we owe the tragic weight of this episode? I think there is an explanation, the only valid one, and that is that Dante felt, in some way, that he was Ulysses. I don't know if he felt it in a conscious way—it doesn't matter. In some tercet of the *Commedia* he says that no one is permitted to know the judgments of Providence. We cannot anticipate them; no one can know who will be saved and who condemned. But Dante has dared, through poetry, to do precisely that. He shows us the condemned and the chosen. He must have known that doing so courted danger. He could not ignore that he was anticipating the indecipherable providence of God.

For this reason the character of Ulysses has such force, because Ulysses is a mirror of Dante, because Dante felt that perhaps he too deserved this punishment. Writing the poem, whether for good or ill, he was infringing on the mysterious laws of the night, of God, of Divinity.

I have reached the end, and again I would like to insist that no one has the right to deprive himself of this pleasure—

the *Commedia*—of reading it in an open way. Later come the commentaries, the desire to know what each mythological allusion means, to see how Dante took a great line of Virgil and perhaps improved it by translating it. In the beginning we must read the book with the faith of a child, abandoning ourselves to it; then it will accompany us to the end. It has accompanied me for so many years, and I know that as soon as I open it tomorrow I will discover things I did not see before. I know that this book will go on, beyond my waking life, and beyond ours.

✥ Nightmares ✥

DREAMS ARE THE genus; nightmares the species. I will speak first of dreams, and then of nightmares.

Lately I've been rereading psychology books, and I have felt singularly defrauded. All of them discuss the mechanisms of dreams or the subjects of dreams, but they do not mention, as I had hoped, that which is so astonishing, so strange—the fact of dreaming.

Thus, in a psychology book I admire greatly, *The Mind of Man*, Gustav Spiller states that dreams correspond to the lowest plane of mental activity—I would maintain that, at least for me, this is an error—and he speaks of the incoherence, the disconnectedness, of the fables of dreams. I would like to recall Paul Groussac and his fine essay, "Among Dreams," in *The Intellectual Voyage*. Groussac writes that it is astonishing that each morning we wake up sane—that is, relatively sane—after having passed through that zone of shades, those labyrinths of dreams.

The study of dreams is particularly difficult, for we cannot examine dreams directly, we can only speak of the memory of dreams. And it is possible that the memory of dreams does not correspond exactly to the dreams themselves. A great writer of the eighteenth century, Sir Thomas Browne, believed that our memory of dreams is more impoverished than the splendor of reality. Others, in turn, believe that we improve our dreams. If we think of the dream as a work of fiction—and I think it is—it may be that we continue to spin tales when we wake and later when we recount them.

I want to recall that great book by Boethius, *De consolatione philosophiae*, which Dante read and reread, as he read and reread all of the literature of the Middle Ages. Boethius, who has been called "the last Roman," Boethius the senator imagined a spectator at a horse race.

The spectator is in the hippodrome, and he sees, from his box, the horses at the starting gate, all the vicissitudes of the race itself, and the arrival of one of the horses at the finishing line. He sees it all in succession. Boethius then imagines another spectator. This other spectator is the spectator of the spectator of the race; he is, let us say, God. God sees the whole race; he sees in a single eternal instant the start, the race, the finish. He sees everything in a single glance; and in the same way he sees all of history. Thus Boethius bridges the concepts of free will and of Providence. Just as the spectator sees the race (albeit sequentially) but does not influence it, so God sees the whole race from cradle to tomb. He does not influence what we do. We act by our own free will, but God knows—God knows at this very moment—our final destiny. God sees all of history, what unfolds as history, in a single splendid dizzying instant that is eternity.

I think now of that book, *An Experiment with Time*—I know no title more interesting—by J. W. Dunne, an English writer of this century. I do not agree with his theory, but it is so beautiful it's worth recalling. In the book he imagines that each one of us possesses a kind of modest personal eternity: one we possess each night. Tonight we will sleep, and tonight, Wednesday night, we will dream. And we will dream of Wednesday and of the next day, Thursday, and perhaps of Friday, and perhaps of Tuesday . . . Each man is given, in dreams, a little personal eternity which allows him to see the recent past and the near future.

All of this the dreamer sees in a single glance, in the same way that God, from His vast eternity, sees the whole cosmic process. And what happens when we wake? What happens is that, as we are accustomed to a sequential life, we give a narrative structure to our dream, though our dream has been multiple and simultaneous.

Let us look at a very simple example. Suppose I dream of a man, simply the image of a man—I'm using a very poor dream—and then, immediately after, I dream the image of a tree. Waking, I can give this dream a complexity it does not have: I can think I have dreamed that a man has been changed into a tree, that he was a tree. Modifying the facts, I spin a tale.

We don't know exactly what happens in dreams. It is not impossible that, during dreams, we are in heaven, we are in hell. Perhaps we are someone, the someone whom Shakespeare called "the thing I am"; perhaps we are ourselves, perhaps we are God. All of this we forget at waking. We can only examine the memory of a dream, the poor memory.

I have read Frazer—a supremely talented writer, but also an extremely credulous one, as it seems he believed everything reported by the various travelers. According to Frazer, savages do not distinguish between waking and dreaming. For them, dreams are episodes of the waking life. Thus, according to Frazer, or according to the travelers he read, a savage dreams he goes into the forest and kills a lion. When he wakes, he thinks his soul has abandoned his body and has killed a lion in his dreams. Or, if we want to complicate things a little, we may suppose that he has killed the dream of a lion. All of this is possible, and this idea of the savages coincides with that of children, who also cannot distinguish between waking and dream.

I will recall a personal memory. A nephew of mine—he was about five or six at the time—used to tell me his dreams each morning. One day, as he was sitting on the floor, I asked him what he had dreamed. Patiently, knowing that I had this *hobby*, he told me: "Last night I dreamed that I was lost in the forest. I was scared, but I came to a clearing, and there was a white house, made of wood, with a staircase that turned around, with steps with runners, and then a door, and out of this door you came out." I interrupted him sharply: "Stop making up things about my house!"

Everything, waking and dream, occurred for him on a single plane. This brings us to another, similar but contrary, hypothesis: that of the mystics and the metaphysicians.

For the savage and for the child, dreams are episodes of the waking life; for poets and mystics, it is not impossible for all of the waking life to be a dream. This was said, in a dry and laconic fashion, by Calderón: "Life is a dream." It was said, with an image, by Shakespeare: "We are such stuff as dreams are made on." And splendidly by the Austrian poet Walter von der Vogelweide, who asked, "*Ist mein Leben geträumt oder ist es wahr?*"—have I dreamed my life or is it real? I am not sure. It takes us certainly to solipsism, to the suspicion that there is only one dreamer and that dreamer is every one of us. That dreamer—let us imagine that I am he—is, at this very moment, dreaming you. He is dreaming this room and this lecture. There is only one dreamer, and that dreamer dreams all of the cosmic process, dreams all of the world's history, dreams everything, including your childhood and your adolescence. All this could not have happened; at this moment it begins to exist. He begins to dream and is each one of us—not *us*, but *each one*. At this moment I am dreaming that I am giving a lecture on the Calle Charcas, that I am looking for things to say (and perhaps not finding them); I am dreaming you. But it is not true. Each one of you is dreaming me and the others.

We have these two ideas: the belief that dreams are part of waking, and the other, the splendid one, the belief of the poets: that all of waking is a dream. There is no difference between the two. It takes us back to Groussac's article: we may be awake, we may be asleep and dreaming, but our mental activity is the same.

There is a passage in the *Odyssey* where it speaks of two gates, one of horn and one of ivory. Through the ivory gate false dreams pass to men, and through the gate of horn go the true and prophetic dreams. And there is a passage in the *Aeneid*, in the sixth book, which has provoked innumerable commentaries. Aeneas descends to the Elysian Fields, beyond the Pillars of Hercules. He speaks with the shades of Achilles and Tiresias; he sees the shade of his mother, he wants to embrace her but cannot because she is made of shadow; and he sees, moreover, the future greatness of the city he will found. He sees Romulus and Remus, a field, and then in that field the future Roman Forum, the future grandeur of Rome, the greatness of Augustus; he sees the whole imperial grandeur. And after having seen all of this, after having talked to its contemporaries (who, for Aeneas, are future people), he returns to the world of the living. What then occurs is quite curious and has never been well explained, except by one anonymous commentator who I believe offered the truth. Aeneas returns through the gate of ivory and not through the gate of horn. Why? The anonymous commentator tells us: because we are not in reality. For Virgil, the real world was possibly the Platonic world, the world of the archetypes. Aeneas passes through the gates of ivory because he enters the world of dreams—that is to say, what we call waking.

Well, all of this may well be.

Now we come to the species, to nightmare. It may be useful to recall the names of nightmare.

The Spanish name, *pesadilla*, is too cheerful: the diminutive *-illa* makes it lack force. In other languages the names are more powerful. In Greek the word is *ephialtes*: Ephialtes is the demon who inspires nightmares. In Latin we have *incubus*. The incubus is the demon who crushes the sleeper, causing the nightmare. In German we have a very curious word, *Alp*, which has come to mean both the elf and the torment brought by elf—the same idea of a demon who inspires nightmares. There is a painting that De Quincey, one of literature's great dreamers of nightmares, saw. It is a painting by Fuseli or Füssli (which was his actual name; he was a Swiss painter of the eighteenth century) called *The Nightmare*. A girl is sleeping. She wakes and is terrified because she sees lying on her belly a monster that is small, black, and malign. This monster is the nightmare. When Fuseli painted this picture he was thinking of the word *Alp*, of the elf's torments.

We come now to the wisest and most ambiguous word, the English *nightmare*, which means the mare of the night. This was how Shakespeare understood it. There is a line of his that says, "I met the night mare." Clearly he saw it as a mare. And there is another line where he says, deliberately, "the nightmare and her nine foals."

But according to the etymologists the root is different. The root is *niht mare* or *niht maere*, the demon of the night. Dr. Johnson, in his famous dictionary, says that this corresponds to Nordic mythology—Saxon mythology we would say—which saw nightmares as the products of demons. This would make it a play on, or translation of, the Greek *ephialtes* or the Latin *incubus*.

There is another interpretation that may help us, one that relates *nightmare* to the German word *Märchen*. *Märchen* means fable, fairy tale, fiction. Nightmare, then, would be the fiction of the night. Whatever the case, the fact of conceiving of nightmare as a mare of the night— there is something terrifying in a mare of the night—was a boon for Victor Hugo. Hugo mastered English and wrote an unjustly forgotten book on Shakespeare. In one of his poems, I think in *Les contemplations*, he speaks of *"le cheval noir de la nuit,"* the black horse of night. No doubt he was thinking of the English word *nightmare*.

We also have the French word, *cauchemar*, which is probably linked to *nightmare*. In all of these words there is an idea of demonic origin, the idea of a demon who causes the nightmare. I believe it does not derive simply from a superstition. I believe that there is—and I speak with complete honesty and sincerity—something true in this idea.

Let us enter into the nightmare, into nightmares. Mine are always the same. I have two nightmares which often become confused with one another. I have the nightmare of the labyrinth, which comes, in part, from a steel engraving I saw in a French book when I was a child. In this engraving were the Seven Wonders of the World, among them the labyrinth of Crete. The labyrinth was a great amphitheater, a very high amphitheater (and this was apparent because it was higher than the cypresses and the men outside it). In this closed structure—ominously closed—there were cracks. I believed when I was a child (or I now believe I believed) that if one had a magnifying glass powerful enough, one could look through the cracks and see the Minotaur in the terrible center of the labyrinth.

My other nightmare is that of the mirror. The two are not distinct, as it only takes two facing mirrors to construct a labyrinth. I remember seeing, in the house of Dora de Alvear in the Belgrano district, a circular room whose walls and doors were mirrored, so that whoever entered the room found himself at the center of a truly infinite labyrinth.

I always dream of labyrinths or of mirrors. In the dream of the mirror another vision appears, another terror of my nights, and that is the idea of the mask. Masks have always scared me. No doubt I felt in my childhood that someone who was wearing a mask was hiding something horrible. These are my most terrible nightmares: I see myself reflected in a mirror, but the reflection is wearing a mask. I am afraid to pull the mask off, afraid to see my real face, which I imagine to be hideous. There may be leprosy or evil or something more terrible than anything I am capable of imagining.

A curious feature of my nightmares—I don't know if you share this with me—is that they have a precise topography. I, for example, always dream of certain corners in Buenos Aires. I'm on the corner of Laprida and Arenales, or the one at Balcarce and Chile. I know exactly where I am, and I know that I must head toward some far-off place. These places in my dreams have a precise topography, but they are completely different. They may be mountain paths or swamps or jungles, it doesn't matter: I know that I am on a certain corner in Buenos Aires. I try to find my way.

Although one might wish otherwise, in dreams what is important is not the images. What matters, as Coleridge said, is the impression produced by the dream. The images are minor; they are effects.

Let us look at a line by Petronius, quoted by Addison. (I am deliberately citing poets, who are particularly illuminating.) He says that, "The soul, without the body, plays." Góngora, in a sonnet, expresses with precision the idea that dreams and nightmares are, above all, fictions; they are literary creations:

> *El sueño, autor de representaciones,*
> *en su teatro sobre el viento armado*
> *sombras suele vestir de bulto bello.*

[The dream, author of representations,| in its
theater above the armored wind| dresses
shadows in beautiful bulk.]

The dream is a representation. Addison reinterpreted the idea according to eighteenth-century principles in an excellent article published in *The Spectator*.

I have cited Sir Thomas Browne. He says that dreams give us an idea of the excellence of the soul, seeing the soul free of the body and engaged in play and dreaming. He thinks that the soul enjoys its freedom. And Addison says effectively that the soul, when it is free of the shackles of the body, imagines, and is able to imagine with a freedom it does not have in waking. He adds that of all the operations of the soul—of the mind we would say, now that we don't use the word *soul*—the most difficult is invention. Yet in dreams we invent so rapidly that we confuse our thoughts with our inventions. We dream we are reading a book, and the truth is we have invented every word in the book. But we don't realize it, and we take it as strange. I have noted in many dreams this anticipatory process, which prepares us for the things to come.

I remember a certain nightmare I had. It took place, I know, on the Calle Serrano, I think at the corner of Serrano and Soler. It did not look like Serrano and Soler—the landscape was quite different—but I *knew* that I was on the old Calle Serrano in the Palermo district. I met a friend, a friend I do not know; I saw him, and he was much changed. I had never seen his face before, but I knew his face could not be like that. He was much changed, and very sad. His face was marked by troubles, by illness, perhaps by guilt. He had his right hand inside his jacket. I couldn't see the hand, which he kept hidden over his heart. I embraced him and felt that I had to help him. "But, my poor Fulano, what has happened? How changed you are!" "Yes," he answered, "I am much changed." Slowly, he withdrew his hand. I could see that it was the claw of a bird.

The strange thing is that from the beginning the man had his hand hidden. Without knowing it, I had paved the way for that invention: that the man had the claw of a bird and that I would see the terrible change, the terrible misfortune, that he was turning into a bird. It also happens in dreams that are not nightmares: they ask us something, and we don't know how to answer; they give us the answer, and we are astonished. The answer may be absurd, but in the dream it is exactly right. Everything has been prepared. I have come to the conclusion, though it may not be scientific, that dreams are the most ancient aesthetic activity.

We know that animals dream. There are Latin verses that speak of the greyhound barking at the hare it chases in dreams. What is curious is the dramatic order of dreams. Addison observed that in the dream we are the theater, the audience, the actors, the plot, the dialogue we hear. We make up everything unconsciously, and everything has a vivacity it does not have in reality. There are people who have weak dreams, vague ones—or, at least, so they tell me. Mine are quite vivid.

Let us return to Coleridge. He says it doesn't matter what we dream, that the dream searches for explanations. He gives an example: a lion suddenly appears in this room, and we all are afraid; the fear has been caused by the image of the lion. But in dreams the reverse can occur. We feel oppressed, and then search for an explanation. I, absurdly but vividly, dream that a sphinx has lain down next to me. The sphinx is not the cause of my fear, it is an explanation of my feeling of oppression. Coleridge adds that people who have been frightened by imaginary ghosts have gone mad. On the other hand, a person who dreams a ghost can wake up and, within a few seconds, regain his composure.

I have had—and I still have—many nightmares. The most terrible, the one that struck me as the most terrible, I used in a sonnet. It went like this: I was in my room; it was dawn (possibly that was the time of the dream). At the foot of my bed was a king, a very ancient king, and I knew in the dream that he was the King of the North, of Norway. He did not look at me; his blind stare was fixed on the ceiling. I felt the terror of his presence. I saw the king, I saw his sword, I saw his dog. Then I woke. But I continued to see the king for a while, because he had made such a strong impression on me. Retold, my dream is nothing; dreamt, it was terrible.

I want to mention a nightmare my friend Susana Bombal recently told me. She dreamed she was in a vaulted room, the top of which was in darkness. From the darkness dropped a black, unraveling piece of cloth. In her hand she awkwardly held a giant pair of scissors. She had to cut the loose threads that hung from the cloth, and they were endless. She kept snipping but she knew she would never finish. And she had the sensation of horror that is the nightmare; for the nightmare is, above all, the sensation of horror.

I have recounted two actual nightmares, and now I will describe two nightmares from literature, which possibly were also real. The first is the *nobile castello* which Dante imagined in the *Inferno*. Dante tells how, guided by Virgil, he reaches the first circle and sees that Virgil has turned pale. He thinks: if Virgil turns pale entering Hell, which is his eternal domain, why do I not feel afraid? He tells this to Virgil, who is terrified. But Virgil says: "I will go first." They go in despair, for they hear around them infinite sighs—not the sighs of physical pain, but the sighs of something more grave.

They come to a noble castle, to the *nobile castello*. It is encircled by seven walls that may be the seven liberal arts of the *trivium* and the *quadrivium* or the seven virtues; it doesn't matter. He speaks of a river that disappears and of a fresh meadow that also disappears. When they reach the meadow, they see that it is enameled, that it is not a living thing. Four shades approach them: the shades of the four great poets of Antiquity. There is Homer, sword in hand; Ovid, Lucan, and Horace. Virgil tells him to greet Homer, whom Dante revered and never read. He tells him, "*Onorate l'altissimo poeta.*" Homer comes forward, sword in hand, and admits Dante as the sixth of the company. Dante, who had still not written the *Commedia* because he was writing it at that moment, knows himself to be capable of writing it.

They then discuss things which Dante does not bother to repeat. We may wonder at the Florentine's modesty, but I think there is a deeper reason. He speaks of those who inhabit the noble castle: there are the great shades of the pagans, and of the Moslems too. They all speak slowly and softly, they have faces of great authority, but they are deprived of God. There is the absence of God. They know they are condemned to that eternal castle, to that castle that is eternal and honorable, but terrible.

There is Aristotle, master of those who know. There are the pre-Socratic philosophers; there is Plato and, alone and apart, the great sultan Saladin. There are all the great pagans who could not be saved because they were never baptized. They could not be saved by Christ, of whom Virgil speaks but cannot name in Hell—he calls him the Mighty One. We may think that Dante had not yet discovered his dramatic talent, he did not yet know that he could make those figures speak. We may lament that Dante does not repeat the great words, no doubt dignified, that Homer, that grand shade, told him, sword in hand. But we may also feel that Dante understood it was better for all to be silent in that terrible castle. Dante merely names them: Seneca, Plato, Aristotle, Saladin, Averroës. He names them, and we don't hear a single word. It's better that way.

I would say, thinking of the *Inferno*, that Hell is not a nightmare; it is simply a torture chamber. Atrocious things take place there, but it does not have the atmosphere of a nightmare that there is in the "noble castle." This is what Dante gives us, perhaps for the first time in literature.

There is another example, one that was praised by De Quincey. It is in the fifth book of Wordsworth's *Prelude*. Wordsworth says that he was preoccupied by the fact that art and science were at the mercy of some cataclysm. (Such a preoccupation was rare at the beginning of the nineteenth century. Today, of course, we think that all of the works of humanity, and humanity itself, could be destroyed in a moment by the atomic bomb.) Well . . . Wordsworth is talking with a friend, and he expresses his horror at the thought that the great works of mankind, the sciences and the arts, could be destroyed. The friend confesses that he too has felt such fears. And Wordsworth says: I have dreamed it . . .

And then comes a dream which seems to me the perfect nightmare, for it contains all the elements of nightmare: episodes of physical ill-being, of persecution, and the element of horror, of the supernatural. Wordsworth tells us that he was in a rocky cave by the sea. It was noon, and he was reading *Don Quixote*, one of his favorite books, "the famous history of the errant knight recorded by Cervantes." He put down the book and began to think about the end of science and art, and then the hour came. The powerful hour of noon, a hot summer noon. "Sleep seized me," he recalls, "and I passed into a dream."

He falls asleep in the cave, facing the sea, amid the golden sands of the beach. In his dream he is also surrounded by sand, a Sahara of black sand. There is no water, there is no sea. He is in the middle of a desert—in the desert one is always in the middle—and he is horrified at the thought of trying to escape. Suddenly he sees there is someone next to him. It is, oddly enough, an Arab of the Bedouin tribes, mounted on a camel and with a lance in his right hand. Under his left arm he has a stone, and in his hand he holds a shell. The Arab tells him that his mission is to save the arts and sciences. He brings the shell to the poet's ear; the shell is of an extraordinary beauty. Wordsworth tells us he hears a prophecy "in an unknown tongue which yet I understood": a sort of tender ode, prophesying that the earth was on the verge of being destroyed by a flood sent by the wrath of God. The Arab tells him that it is true, the flood is coming, but that he has a mission: to save the arts and sciences. He shows him the stone. And the stone is, curiously, Euclid's *Elements*, while remaining a stone. Then he brings the shell closer, and the shell too is a book; it is what had spoken those terrible things. The shell is, moreover, all the poetry of the world, including—why not?—the poem by Wordsworth. The Bedouin tells him that he must save these two things, the stone and the shell, both of them books. He turns around, and there is a moment in which Wordsworth sees that the face of the Bedouin has changed, that it is full of horror. He too turns around, and he sees a great light, a light that has now flooded the middle of the desert. It is the waters of the flood that will destroy the earth. The Bedouin goes off, and Wordsworth sees that the Bedouin is also Don Quixote and that the camel is also Rosinante and that, in the same way that the stone was a book and the shell a book, so the Bedouin is Don Quixote and is neither of the two and is both at once. This duality corresponds to the horror of the dream. Wordsworth, at that moment, wakes with a cry of terror, for the waters have engulfed him.

I think that this nightmare is one of the most beautiful in literature.

We may draw two conclusions, at least tonight; later we can change our minds. The first is that dreams are an aesthetic work, perhaps the most ancient aesthetic expression. They take a strangely dramatic form. We are, as Addison said, the theater, the spectators, the actors, the story. The second refers to the horror of nightmares. Our waking life abounds in terrible moments; we all know that there are moments in which reality overwhelms us. A loved one has died, a loved one has left us; such are the causes of sadness, of despair . . . Nevertheless, these do not pertain to nightmares. The nightmare has a particular horror, and that horror may be expressed by any story. It may be expressed by Wordsworth's Bedouin who is also Don

Quixote, by scissors and threads, by my dream of the king, by the famous nightmares of Poe. But there is something: it is the *flavor* of the nightmare. In the treatises I have consulted they do not speak of this horror.

We also have the possibility of a theological interpretation, one that would be in accord with etymology. Take any of the words: the Latin *incubus*, the Saxon *nightmare*, the German *Alp*. All of them suggest something supernatural. Well, what if nightmares were strictly supernatural? What if nightmares were cries from hell? What if nightmares literally took place in hell? Why not? Everything is so strange that even this is possible.

The Thousand and One Nights

A MAJOR EVENT in the history of the West was the discovery of the East. It would be more precise to speak of a continuing consciousness of the East, comparable to the presence of Persia in Greek history. Within this general consciousness of the Orient—something vast, immobile, magnificent, incomprehensible—there were certain high points, and I would like to mention a few. This seems to me the best approach to a subject I love so much, one I have loved since childhood, *The Book of the Thousand and One Nights* or, as it is called in the English version—the one I first read—*The Arabian Nights*, a title that is not without mystery, but is less beautiful.

I will mention a few of these high points. First, the nine books of Herodotus, and in them the revelation of Egypt, far-off Egypt. I say "far-off" because space was measured by time, and the journey was hazardous. For the Greeks, the Egyptian world was older and greater, and they felt it to be mysterious.

We will examine later the words *Orient* and *Occident*, *East* and *West*, which we cannot define, but which are true. They remind me of what St. Augustine said about time: "What is time? If you don't ask me, I know; but if you ask me, I don't know." What are the East and the West? If you ask me, I don't know. We must settle for approximations.

Let us look at the encounters, the campaigns, and the wars of Alexander, who conquered Persia and India and who died finally in Babylonia, as everyone knows. This was the first great meeting with the East, an encounter that so affected Alexander that he ceased to be Greek and became partly Persian. The Persians have now incorporated him into their history—Alexander, who slept with a sword and the *Iliad* under his pillow. We will return to him later, but since we are mentioning Alexander, I would like to recall a legend that may be of interest to you.

Alexander does not die in Babylonia at age thirty-three. He is separated from his men and wanders through the deserts and forests, and at last he sees a great light. It is a bonfire, and it is surrounded by warriors with yellow skin and slanted eyes. They do not know him; they welcome him. As he is at heart a soldier, he joins in battles in a geography that is unknown to him. He is a soldier: the causes do not matter to him, but he is willing to die for them. The years pass, and he has forgotten many things. Finally the day arrives when the troops are paid off, and among the coins there is one that disturbs him. He has it in the palm of his hand, and he says: "You are an old man; this is the medal that was struck for the victory of Arbela when I was Alexander of Macedon." At that moment he remembers his past, and he returns to being a mercenary for the Tartars or Chinese or whoever they were.

That memorable invention belongs to the poet Robert Graves. To Alexander had been prophesied the dominion of the East and the West. The Islamic countries still honor him under the name Alexander the Two-Horned, because he ruled the two horns of East and West.

Let us look at another example of this great—and not infrequently, tragic—dialogue between East and West. Let us think of the young Virgil, touching a piece of printed silk from a distant country. The country of the Chinese, of which he only knows that it is far-off and peaceful, at the furthest reaches of the Orient. Virgil will remember that silk in his *Georgics*, that seamless silk, with images of temples, emperors, rivers, bridges, and lakes far removed from those he knew.

Another revelation of the Orient is that admirable book, the *Natural History* of Pliny. There he speaks of the Chinese, and he mentions Bactria, Persia, and the India of King Porus. There is a poem of Juvenal I read more than forty years ago, which suddenly comes to mind. In order to speak of a far-off place, Juvenal says "*ultra Auroram et Gangem,*" beyond the dawn and the Ganges. In those four words is, for us, the East. Who knows if Juvenal felt it as we do? I think so. The East has always held a fascination for the people of the West.

Proceeding through history, we reach a curious gift. Possibly it never happened; it has sometimes been considered a legend. Harun al-Rashid, Aaron the Orthodox, sent his counterpart Charlemagne an elephant. Perhaps it was impossible to send an elephant from Baghdad to France, but that is not important. It doesn't hurt to believe it. That elephant is a monster. Let us remember that the word *monster* does not mean something horrible. Lope de Vega was called a "Monster of Nature" by Cervantes. That elephant must have been something quite strange for the French and for the Germanic king Charlemagne. (It is sad to think that Charlemagne could not have read the *Chanson de Roland*, for he spoke some Germanic dialect.)

They sent the elephant, and that word *elephant* reminds us that Roland sounded the *olifant*, the ivory trumpet that got its name precisely because it came from the tusk of an elephant. And since we are speaking of etymologies, let us recall that the Spanish word *alfil*, the bishop in the game of chess, means elephant in Arabic and has the same origin as *marfil*, ivory. Among Oriental chess pieces I have seen an elephant with a castle and a little man. That piece was not the rook, as one might think from the castle, but rather the bishop, the *alfil* or elephant.

In the Crusades, the soldiers returned and brought back memories. They brought memories of lions, for example. We have the famous crusader Richard the Lion-Hearted. The lion that entered into heraldry is an animal from the East. This list should not go on forever, but let us remember Marco Polo, whose book is a revelation of the Orient—for a long time it was the major source. The book was dictated to a friend in jail, after the battle in which the Venetians were conquered by the Genoese. In it, there is the history of the Orient, and he speaks of Kublai Khan, who will reappear in a certain poem by Coleridge.

In the fifteenth century in the city of Alexandria, the city of Alexander the Two-Horned, a series of tales was gathered. Those tales have a strange history, as it is generally believed. They were first told in India, then in Persia, then in Asia Minor, and finally were written down in Arabic and compiled in Cairo. They became *The Book of the Thousand and One Nights*.

I want to pause over the title. It is one of the most beautiful in the world, as beautiful, I think, as that other title I have mentioned, *An Experiment with Time*.

In this, there is another kind of beauty. I think it lies in the fact that for us the word *thousand* is almost synonymous with *infinite*. To say *a thousand nights* is to say infinite nights, countless nights, endless nights. To say *a thousand and one nights* is to add one to infinity. Let us recall a curious English expression: instead of *forever*, they sometimes say *forever and a day*. A day has been added to forever. It is reminiscent of a line of Heine, written to a woman: "I will love you eternally and even after."

The idea of infinity is consubstantial with *The Thousand and One Nights*.

In 1704, the first European version was published, the first of the six volumes by the French Orientalist Antoine Galland. With the Romantic movement, the Orient richly entered the consciousness of Europe. It is enough to mention two great names: Byron, more important for his image than for his work, and Hugo, the greatest of them all. By 1890 or so, Kipling could say: "Once you have heard the call of the East, you will never hear anything else."

Let us return for a moment to the first translation of *The Thousand and One Nights*. It is a major event for all of European literature. We are in 1704, in France. It is the France of the Grand Siècle; it is the France where literature is legislated by Boileau, who dies in 1711 and never suspects that all of his rhetoric is threatened by that splendid Oriental invasion.

Let us think about the rhetoric of Boileau, made of precautions and prohibitions, of the cult of reason and of that beautiful line of Fénelon: "Of the operations of the spirit, the least frequent is reason." Boileau, of course, wanted to base poetry on reason.

We are speaking in the illustrious dialect of Latin we call Spanish, and it too is an episode of that nostalgia, of that amorous and at times bellicose commerce between Orient and Occident, for the discovery of America is due to the desire to reach the Indies. We call the people of Moctezuma and Atahualpa *Indians* precisely because of this error, because the Spaniards believed they had reached the Indies.

This little lecture is part of that dialogue between East and West.

As for the word *Occident*, we know its origin, but that does not matter. Suffice to say that Western culture is not pure in the sense that it exists entirely because of Western efforts. Two nations have been essential for our culture: Greece (since Rome is a Hellenistic extension) and Israel, an Eastern country. Both are combined into what we call Western civilization. Speaking of the revelations of the East, we must also remember the continuing revelation that is the Holy Scripture. The fact is reciprocal, now that the West influences the East. There is a book by a French author called *The Discovery of Europe by the Chinese*— that too must have occurred.

The Orient is the place where the sun comes from. There is a beautiful German word for the East, *Morgenland*, the land of morning. For the West it is *Abendland*, land of afternoon. You will recall Spengler's *Der Untergang des Abendlandes*, that is, *the downward motion of the land of afternoon*, or, as it is translated more prosaically, *The Decline of the West*. I think that we must not renounce the word *Orient*, a word so beautiful, for within it, by happy chance, is the word *oro*, gold. In the word *Orient* we feel the word *oro*, for when the sun rises we see a sky of gold. I come back to that famous line of Dante: "*Dolce color d'oriental zaffiro.*" The word *oriental* here has two meanings: the Oriental sapphire, which comes from the East, and also the gold of morning, the gold of that first morning in Purgatory.

What is the Orient? If we attempt to define it in a geographical way, we encounter something quite strange: part of the Orient, North Africa, is in the West, or what for the Greeks and Romans was the West. Egypt is also the

Orient, and the lands of Israel, Asia Minor, and Bactria, Persia, India—all of those countries that stretch further and further and have little in common with one another. Thus, for example, Tartary, China, Japan—all of that is our Orient. Hearing the word *Orient*, I think we all think, first of all, of the Islamic Orient, and by extension the Orient of northern India.

Such is the primary meaning it has for us, and this is the product of *The Thousand and One Nights*. There is something we feel as the Orient, something I have not felt in Israel but have felt in Granada and in Córdoba. I have felt the presence of the East, and I don't know if I can define it; perhaps it's not worth it to define something we feel instinctively. The connotations of that word we owe to *The Thousand and One Nights*. It is our first thought; only later do we think of Marco Polo or the legends of Prester John, of those rivers of sand with fishes of gold. First we think of Islam.

Let us look at the history of the book, and then at the translations. The origin of the book is obscure. We may think of the cathedrals, miscalled Gothic, that are the works of generations of men. But there is an essential difference: the artisans and craftsmen of the cathedrals knew what they were making. In contrast, *The Thousand and One Nights* appears in a mysterious way. It is the work of thousands of authors, and none of them knew that he was helping to construct this illustrious book, one of the most illustrious books in all literature (and one more appreciated in the West than in the East, so they tell me).

Now, a curious note that was transcribed by the Baron von Hammer-Purgstall, an Orientalist cited with admiration by both Lane and Burton, the two most famous English translators of *The Thousand and One Nights*. He speaks of certain men he calls *confabulatores nocturni*, men of the night who tell stories, men whose profession it is to tell stories during the night. He cites an ancient Persian text which states that the first person to hear such stories told, who gathered the men of the night to tell stories in order to ease his insomnia, was Alexander of Macedon.

Those stories must have been fables. I suspect that the enchantment of fables is not in their moral. What enchanted Aesop or the Hindu fabulists was to imagine animals that were like little men, with their comedies and tragedies. The idea of the moral proposition was added later. What was important was the fact that the wolf spoke with the sheep and the ox with the ass, or the lion with the nightingale.

We have Alexander of Macedon hearing the stories told by these anonymous men of the night, and this profession lasted for a long time. Lane, in his book *Account of the Manners and Customs of the Modern Egyptians*, says that as late as 1850 storytellers were common in Cairo. There were some fifty of them, and they often told stories from *The Thousand and One Nights*.

We have a series of tales. Those from India, which form the central core (according to Burton and to Cansinos-Asséns, author of an excellent Spanish version) pass on to Persia; in Persia they are modified, enriched, and Arabized. They finally reach Egypt, at the end of the fifteenth century, and the first compilation is made. This one leads to another, apparently Persian version: *Hazar Afsana*, the thousand tales.

Why were there first a thousand and later a thousand and one? I think there are two reasons. First, there was the superstition—and superstition is very important in this case —that even numbers are evil omens. They then sought an odd number and luckily added *and one*. If they had made it nine hundred and ninety-nine we would have felt that there was a night missing. This way we feel that we have been given something infinite, that we have received a bonus, another night.

We know that chronology and history exist, but they are primarily Western discoveries. There are no Persian histories of literature or Indian histories of philosophy, nor are there Chinese histories of Chinese literature, because they are not interested in the succession of facts. They believe that literature and poetry are eternal processes. I think they are basically right. For example, the title *The Book of the Thousand and One Nights* would be beautiful even if it were invented this morning. If it had been made today we would think what a lovely title, and it is lovely not only because it is beautiful (as beautiful as Lugones' *Los crepúsculos del jardın*, the twilights of the garden) but because it makes you want to read the book.

One feels like getting lost in *The Thousand and One Nights*, one knows that entering that book one can forget one's own poor human fate; one can enter a world, a world made up of archetypal figures but also of individuals.

In the title *The Thousand and One Nights* there is something very important: the suggestion of an infinite book. It practically is. The Arabs say that no one can read *The Thousand and One Nights* to the end. Not for reasons of boredom: one feels the book is infinite.

At home I have the seventeen volumes of Burton's version. I know I'll never read all of them, but I know that there the nights are waiting for me; that my life may be wretched but the seventeen volumes will be there; there will be that species of eternity, *The Thousand and One Nights* of the Orient.

How does one define the Orient (not the real Orient, which does not exist)? I would say that the notions of East and West are generalizations, but that no individual can feel himself to be Oriental. I suppose that a man feels himself to be Persian or Hindu or Malaysian, but not Oriental. In the same way, no one feels himself to be Latin American: we feel ourselves to be Argentines or Chileans. It doesn't matter; the concept does not exist.

What is the Orient, then? It is above all a world of extremes in which people are very unhappy or very happy, very rich or very poor. A world of kings, of kings who do not have to explain what they do. Of kings who are, we might say, as irresponsible as gods.

There is, moreover, the notion of hidden treasures. Anybody may discover one. And the notion of magic, which is very important. What is magic? Magic is a unique causality. It is the belief that besides the causal relations we know, there is another causal relation. That relationship may be due to accidents, to a ring, to a lamp. We rub a ring, a lamp, and a genie appears. That genie is a slave who is also omnipotent and who will fulfill our wishes. It can happen at any moment.

Let us recall the story of the fisherman and the genie. The fisherman has four children and is poor. Every morning he casts his net from the banks of a sea. Already the expression *a sea* is magical, placing us in a world of undefined geography. The fisherman doesn't go down to *the* sea, he goes down to *a* sea and casts his net. One morning he casts and hauls it in three times: he hauls in a dead donkey, he hauls in broken pots—in short, useless things. He casts his net a fourth time—each time he recites a poem—and the net is very heavy. He hopes it will be full of fish, but what he hauls in is a jar of yellow copper, sealed with the seal of Suleiman (Solomon). He opens the jar, and a thick smoke emerges. He thinks of selling the jar to the hardware merchants, but the smoke rises to the sky, condenses, and forms the figure of a genie.

What are these genies? They are related to a pre-Adamite creation—before Adam, inferior to men, but they can be gigantic. According to the Moslems, they inhabit all of space and are invisible and impalpable.

The genie says, "All praises to God and Solomon His Prophet." The fisherman asks why he speaks of Solomon, who died so long ago; today His Prophet is Mohammed. He also asks him why he is closed up in the jar. The genie tells him that he was one of those who rebelled against Solomon, and that Solomon enclosed him in the jar, sealed it, and threw it to the bottom of the sea. Four hundred years passed, and the genie pledged that whoever liberated him would be given all the gold in the world. Nothing happened. He swore that whoever liberated him, he would teach the song of the birds. The centuries passed, and the promises multiplied. Finally he swore that he would kill whoever freed him. "Now I must fulfill my promise. Prepare to die, my savior!" That flash of rage makes the genie strangely human, and perhaps likable.

The fisherman is terrified. He pretends to disbelieve the story, and he says: "What you have told me cannot be true. How could you, whose head touches the sky and whose feet touch the earth, fit into that tiny jar?" The genie answers: "Man of little faith, you will see." He shrinks, goes back into the jar, and the fisherman seals it up.

The story continues, and the protagonist becomes not a fisherman but a king, then the king of the Black Islands, and at the end everything comes together. It is typical of *The*

Thousand and One Nights. We may think of those Chinese spheres in which there are other spheres, or of Russian dolls. We encounter something similar in *Don Quixote* but not taken to the extremes of *The Thousand and One Nights*. Moreover, all of this is inside of a vast central tale which you all know: that of the sultan who has been deceived by his wife and who, in order never to be deceived again, resolves to marry every night and kill the woman the following morning. Until Scheherazade pledges to save the others and stays alive by telling stories that remain unfinished. They spend a thousand and one nights together, and in the end she produces a son.

Stories within stories create a strange effect, almost infinite, a sort of vertigo. This has been imitated by writers ever since. Thus the "Alice" books of Lewis Carroll or his novel *Sylvia and Bruno*, where there are dreams that branch out and multiply.

The subject of dreams is a favorite of *The Thousand and One Nights*. For example, the story of the two dreamers. A man in Cairo dreams that a voice orders him to go to Isfahan in Persia, where a treasure awaits him. He undertakes the long and difficult voyage and finally reaches Isfahan. Exhausted, he stretches out in the patio of a mosque to rest. Without knowing it, he is among thieves. They are all arrested, and the cadi asks him why he has come to the city. The Egyptian tells him. The cadi laughs until he shows the back of his teeth and says to him: "Foolish and gullible man, three times I have dreamed of a house in Cairo, behind which is a garden, and in the garden a sundial, and then a fountain and a fig tree, and beneath the fountain there is a treasure. I have never given the least credit to this lie. Never return to Isfahan. Take this money and go." The man returns to Cairo. He has recognized his own house in the cadi's dream. He digs beneath the fountain and finds the treasure.

In *The Thousand and One Nights* there are echoes of the West. We encounter the adventures of Ulysses, except that Ulysses is called Sinbad the Sailor. The adventures are at times identical: for example, the story of Polyphemus.

To erect the palace of *The Thousand and One Nights* it took generations of men, and those men are our benefactors, as we have inherited this inexhaustible book, this book capable of so much metamorphosis. I say so much metamorphosis because the first translation, that of Galland, is quite simple and is perhaps the most enchanting of them all, the least demanding on the reader. Without this first text, as Captain Burton said, the later versions could not have been written.

Galland publishes his first volume in 1704. It produces a sort of scandal, but at the same time it enchants the rational France of Louis XIV. When we think of the Romantic movement, we usually think of dates that are much later. But it might be said that the Romantic movement begins at that moment when someone, in Normandy or in Paris, reads *The Thousand and One Nights*. He leaves the world legislated by Boileau and enters the world of Romantic freedom.

The other events come later: the discovery of the picaresque novel by the Frenchman Le Sage; the Scots and English ballads published by Percy around 1750; and, around 1798, the Romantic movement beginning in England with Coleridge, who dreams of Kublai Khan, the protector of Marco Polo. We see how marvelous the world is and how interconnected things are.

Then come the other translations. The one by Lane is accompanied by an encyclopedia of the customs of the

Moslems. The anthropological and obscene translation by Burton is written in a curious English partly derived from the fourteenth century, an English full of archaisms and neologisms, an English not devoid of beauty but which at times is difficult to read. Then the licensed (in both senses of the word) version of Doctor Mardrus, and a German version, literal but without literary charm, by Littmann. Now, happily, we have a Spanish version by my teacher Rafael Cansinos-Asséns. The book has been published in Mexico; it is perhaps the best of all the versions, and it is accompanied by notes.

The most famous tale of *The Thousand and One Nights* is not found in the original version. It is the story of Aladdin and the magic lamp. It appears in Galland's version, and Burton searched in vain for an Arabic or Persian text. Some have suspected that Galland forged the tale. I think the word *forged* is unjust and malign. Galland had as much right to invent a story as did those *confabulatores nocturni.* Why shouldn't we suppose that after having translated so many tales, he wanted to invent one himself, and did?

The story does not end with Galland. In his auto-biography De Quincey says that, for him, there was one story in *The Thousand and One Nights* that was incomparably superior to the others, and that was the story of Aladdin. He speaks of the magician of Magreb who comes to China because he knows that there is the one person capable of exhuming the marvelous lamp. Galland tells us that the magician was an astrologer, and that the stars told him he had to go to China to find the boy. De Quincey, who had a wonderfully inventive memory, records a completely different fact. According to him, the magician had put his ear to the ground and had heard the innumerable footsteps of men. And he had distinguished, from among the footsteps, those of the boy destined to discover the lamp. This, said De Quincey, brought him to the idea that the world is made of correspondences, is full of magic mirrors—that in small things is the cipher of the large. The fact of the magician putting his ear to the ground and deciphering the footsteps of Aladdin appears in none of these texts. It is an invention of the memory or the dreams of De Quincey.

The Thousand and One Nights has not died. The infinite time of the thousand and one nights continues its course. At the beginning of the eighteenth century the book was translated; at the beginning of the nineteenth (or end of the eighteenth) De Quincey remembered it another way. The *Nights* will have other translators, and each translator will create a different version of the book. We may almost speak of the many books titled *The Thousand and One Nights*: two in French, by Galland and Mardrus; three in English, by Burton, Lane, and Paine; three in German, by Henning, Littmann, and Weil; one in Spanish, by Cansinos-Asséns. Each of these books is different, because *The Thousand and One Nights* keeps growing or recreating itself. Stevenson's admirable *New Arabian Nights* takes up the subject of the disguised prince who walks through the city accompanied by his vizier and who has curious adventures. But Stevenson invented his prince, Floricel of Bohemia, and his aide-de-camp, Colonel Geraldine, and he had them walk through London. Not a real London, but a London similar to Baghdad; not the Baghdad of reality, but the Baghdad of *The Thousand and One Nights*.

There is another author we must add: Chesterton, Stevenson's heir. The fantastic London in which occur the adventures of Father Brown and of The Man Who Was Thursday would not exist if he hadn't read Stevenson. And

Stevenson would not have written his *New Arabian Nights* if he hadn't read *The Arabian Nights*. *The Thousand and One Nights* is not something which has died. It is a book so vast that it is not necessary to have read it, for it is a part of our memory—and also, now, a part of tonight.

✣ Buddhism ✣

THE SUBJECT TONIGHT is Buddhism. I will not go into the long history that begins some twenty-five hundred years ago in Benares, when a prince of Nepal named Siddhartha or Gautama became the Buddha, set in motion the wheel of the Law, and proclaimed the four noble truths and the eight-fold path. I will speak of the essence of the religion, the elements of Buddhism which have been preserved since the fifth century before Christ. From the age of Heraclitus, Pythagoras, and Zeno, up to our own time, the elements have remained the same, but the religion has become encrusted with mythology, astronomy, extraneous beliefs, and magic. Since the subject is complex, I will limit myself to what the diverse sects have in common. This corresponds, more or less, to Hinayana, or the Lesser Vehicle.

Let us consider first the longevity of Buddhism. This may be explained by historical reasons, but they are, at best, fortuitous and debatable. I think there are two fundamental causes. The first is the extraordinary tolerance of Buddhism, which does not pertain, as is the case of other religions, to certain periods: Buddhism has always been tolerant.

It has never resorted to iron or to fire; it has never believed that these means could be persuasive. When Ashoka, emperor of India, became a Buddhist, he did not try to impose his new religion on anyone. A good Buddhist can be a Lutheran or Methodist or Presbyterian or Calvinist or Shintoist or Taoist or Catholic; he may be a proselyte of Islam or of the Jewish religion, all with complete freedom. In contrast, it is not permissible for a Christian, a Jew, or a Moslem to be Buddhist.

The tolerance of Buddhism is not a weakness but rather part of its particular disposition. Buddhism is, above all, what could be called a *yoga*. What is *yoga*? It is the same word as *yoke*, which has its origin in the Latin *iugum*—a yoke, a discipline man imposes on himself. If we understand what the Buddha preached in that first sermon in the Deer Park in Benares twenty-five hundred years ago, we may understand Buddhism. Except that one does not attempt to understand it, one attempts to feel it in a deep way, to feel it in body and soul—except, of course, that Buddhism does not admit the reality of the body or of the soul.

There is a second reason for its longevity. Buddhism requires a greal deal of faith. This is natural, as all religion is an act of faith. So too is patriotism an act of faith. I have often asked myself, what does it mean to be Argentine? To be Argentine is to feel that we are Argentines. What does it mean to be Buddhist? To be Buddhist is—not to understand, because that can be accomplished in a few minutes— but to *feel* the four noble truths and the eightfold path.

Then there is the story of the Buddha. We may, if we like, not believe that story. I have a Japanese friend, a Zen Buddhist, with whom I've had long and friendly discussions. I told him I believed in the historical reality of the Buddha. I believed, and still believe, that some twenty-five hundred years ago there was a prince of Nepal named Siddhartha or Gautama who became the Buddha, the Enlightened or

Awakened One—as opposed to the rest of us who are sleeping or are dreaming this great dream that is life. I remember that line of Joyce: "History is a nightmare from which I am trying to awake." Well, Siddhartha, at age thirty, woke up and became the Buddha.

I talked with my friend who was a Buddhist—I'm not sure I'm a Christian, but I am sure that I'm not a Buddhist— and I said: "Why not believe in the story of Prince Siddhartha?" He replied: "Because it doesn't matter; what matters is to believe in the Teachings." He added, I think with more wit than truth, that to believe in the historical existence of the Buddha, or to be interested in it, is something like confusing the laws of mathematics with the biographies of Pythagoras or Newton. One of the subjects of meditation for the monks in the monasteries of China and Japan is to doubt the existence of the Buddha. It is one of the doubts that must be imposed on one's self in order to arrive at the truth.

The other religions require a great deal of credulity. If we are Christians, we must believe that one of the three figures of the Divinity condescended to become a man and was crucified in Judaea. If we are Moslems, we must believe that there is no other god but God and that Mohammed is His prophet. But we can be good Buddhists and deny the Buddha's existence. Or, more exactly, we must know that our belief in the historical is not important; what is important is to believe in the Teachings. Nevertheless, the legend of the Buddha is so beautiful I can't help but mention it.

The French have given particular attention to the study of the legend of the Buddha. Their argument is this: the biography of the Buddha relates what happened to one man in a brief period of time. It may or may not have happened that way. In contrast, the legend of the Buddha has illuminated and continues to illuminate millions of people. The legend is what has inspired so many beautiful paintings, sculptures, and poems. Buddhism, besides being a religion, is a mythology, a cosmology, a metaphysical system—or more exactly, a series of metaphysical systems which do not recognize each other and which dispute among themselves.

Although one need not believe it, the legend of the Buddha is illuminating. It begins in the heavens. In the heavens there is someone who for centuries and centuries— we may literally say for an infinite number of centuries— has been perfecting himself toward understanding, and who, in his next incarnation, will be the Buddha.

He chooses the continent in which he will be born. According to Buddhist cosmogony, the world is divided into four triangular continents and in the center is a mountain of gold, Mt. Meru. He will be born in what corresponds to India. He chooses the century in which he will be born; he chooses his caste, his mother.

Now the terrestrial part of the legend. There is a queen, Maya, married to the king Suddhodana. *Maya* means illusion. She dreams that a white elephant with six tusks, who wandered in the mountains of gold, enters her left side without causing pain. She wakes. The king gathers his astrologers, and they explain that the queen will give birth to a son who will become either the emperor of the earth or the Buddha, the Enlightened or Awakened One, the being destined to save all mankind. As might be expected, the king prefers the first destiny: he wants his son to be emperor of the earth.

Let us go back to the detail of the white elephant with the six tusks. Oldenberg has noted that the elephant in India is a common domestic animal. The color white is always the symbol of innocence. Why six tusks? We must remember (it recurs at times in history) that the number six, which for us is arbitrary or inconvenient—we prefer three or seven—is not random in India. They believe that there are six dimensions in space: above, below, in front, behind, left, right. A white elephant with six tusks is not extravagant for Hindus.

The king gathers his magicians, and the queen painlessly gives birth. A fig tree bends its branches to help her. The child is born standing, and at birth he takes four steps— north, south, east, and west—and speaks with the voice of a lion: "I am the incomparable; this will be my last birth." (The Hindus believe in an infinite number of births.) The prince grows up to be the best archer, the best horseman, the best swimmer, the best athelete, the best calligrapher; he confounds all the doctors (here we may think of Christ and the doctors). At sixteen he marries.

The father knows—the astrologers have told him—that his son runs the risk of becoming the Buddha, the man who will save the others, if he learns four facts of life: old age, sickness, death, and asceticism. He secludes his son in the palace and provides him with a harem. I will not mention the number of women, obviously a Hindu exaggeration. Well, why not say it? There were eighty-four thousand.

The prince lives a happy life. He doesn't know there is suffering in the world; he has been protected from old age, sickness, death. On the predestined day he goes out in his coach through one of the four gates of the rectangular palace; let us say through the north gate. He travels for a while and then he sees a creature different from anything he has ever seen. It is stooped over, wrinkled; it has no hair. It can barely walk and leans on a staff. He asks who the man is, if he is indeed a man. The coachman answers that he is an old man and that we will all be that man if we keep on living.

The prince returns to the palace, troubled. Six days later he again goes out, this time through the south gate. He sees in a ditch a man who is even stranger: one with the disfigured face of a leper. He asks who that man is, if he is a man. He is a sick man, the coachman replies. We will all be that man if we keep on living.

The prince, now quite disturbed, returns to the palace. Six days later he leaves again, and he sees a man who seems to be sleeping but whose color is not that of life. The man is being carried by others. He asks who he is. The coachman tells him that this is a dead man and we will all be that dead man when we have lived long enough.

The prince is desolate. Three horrible truths have been revealed to him: the truth of old age, the truth of sickness, the truth of death. He goes out a fourth time. He sees a man who is almost naked and whose face is full of serenity. He asks who he is. They tell him that the man is an ascetic, a man who has renounced everything and who has gained beatitude.

The prince resolves to give up everything—he, who has had a life so rich. (Buddhism believes that asceticism may be necessary but only after having tried life. It does not believe that one must begin by denying everything. One must purify one's life down to the dregs and then renounce the illusion of life, but not without first knowing it.) The prince resolves to be a Buddha. At this moment they bring him a message: his wife, Yashodhara, has given birth to a child. He says: "A fetter has been forged." It is the son who chains him to life. For this reason he names him Rahula, which means *fetter*. Siddhartha is in his harem, looking at these women who are young and beautiful, and he sees horrible, leprous old women. He goes to his wife's room. She is sleeping. He takes the child in his arms. He is about to kiss his wife, but he knows that if he kisses her he will not be able to give her up, and he leaves.

He seeks out various teachers. The teachers instruct him in asceticism, which he practices for a long time. At the end, he is lying in the middle of a field; his body is immobile, and the gods who see him from the thirty-three heavens think he is dead. One of them, the wisest, says, "No, he has not died. He will be the Buddha." The prince wakes, crosses a nearby stream, takes a little food, and sits beneath the sacred pipal tree—what might be called the tree of the Law.

What follows next is a magical interlude, one which corresponds to the Gospels: the fight with the demon. The demon here is called Mara. (We have already seen that word *nightmare*, demon of the night.) Mara feels that her dominion over the world has been threatened, and she leaves her palace. The strings of her musical instruments have broken; the water has dried up in her tanks. She gathers her troops, mounts an elephant I don't know how many thousands of feet high, multiplies her arms and her weapons, and attacks the prince. The prince is seated in the late afternoon beneath the tree of knowledge, the tree that was born at the same time as he.

The demon and her army of tigers, lions, camels, elephants, and monstrous warriors shoot arrows at the prince. They turn into flowers. They hurl mountains of fire, and the flames form a canopy over his head. The prince meditates, immobile, with his legs crossed. Perhaps he doesn't know that he is being attacked. He thinks on life; he is reaching Nirvana, salvation. Before the sun sets, the demon has been defeated. A long night of meditation follows; at the end of it, Siddhartha is no longer Siddhartha. He is the Buddha; he has reached Nirvana.

He resolves to teach the Law. He rises—now that he has been saved he wants to save the others. He delivers his first sermon in the Deer Park in Benares. Then he gives another sermon, the Fire Sermon, in which he says that everything is burning: souls, bodies, all is on fire. (At more or less the same time, Heraclitus of Ephesus was also saying that everything is fire.)

His Law is not that of asceticism, since for the Buddha asceticism is an error. Man need not abandon the carnal life because it is lowly, ignoble, shameful, sorrowful; asceticism too is ignoble and sorrowful. He preaches a middle way—to use the theological terminology. He has reached Nirvana, and he continues to live for another forty-odd years, dedicated to teaching. He could have remained immortal, but he chooses the moment of his death, after he has gathered many disciples.

He is dying in the house of a blacksmith. His disciples surround him. They are in despair. What will they do without him? He tells them that he does not exist, that he too is a man, as unreal and as mortal as they, but that he is leaving them the Law. Here is a great difference from Christ. Jesus told his disciples that if two are gathered, he will be the third. In contrast, the Buddha says: I leave you my Law. That is to say, he has, with the first sermon, put into motion the wheel of the Law. Later will come the history of Buddhism: lamaism, magical Buddhism, Hinayana or the Lesser Vehicle, Mahayana or the Greater Vehicle, the Zen Buddhism of Japan.

To my mind, the form of Buddhism most similar, practically identical, to what the Buddha taught is Zen.

The others are mythological encrustations, fables. It is known that the Buddha could perform miracles. But, like Jesus, miracles displeased him; he disliked performing them. They seemed to him a vulgar ostentation. There is a story I will tell: that of the sandalwood bowl.

A merchant in a city of India carves a piece of sandalwood into a bowl. He places it at the top of some bamboo stalks which are high and very slippery and declares that he will give the bowl to whomever can fetch it. Some heretical teachers try in vain. They then attempt to bribe the merchant to say they had succeeded. The merchant refuses, and a minor disciple of the Buddha arrives. (His name is not mentioned outside of this incident.) The disciple rises through the air, flies six times around the bowl, picks it up, and delivers it to the merchant. When the Buddha hears the story he expels the disciple from the order for indulging in something so frivolous.

But the Buddha also performed miracles. For example this one, a miracle of courtesy: The Buddha has to cross a desert at noon. The gods, from their thirty-three heavens, each send him down a parasol. The Buddha does not want to slight any of the gods, so he turns himself into thirty-three Buddhas. Each god sees a Buddha protected by the parasol he sent.

Among the stories of the Buddha, there is one that is particularly illuminating: the parable of the arrow. A man has been wounded in battle, but he does not want them to remove the arrow. First he wants to know the name of the archer, to what caste he belongs, what the arrow is made of, where the archer was standing at the time, how long the arrow is. While he is discussing these things, he dies. "I, however," said the Buddha, "teach that one must pull the arrow out." What is the arrow? It is the universe. The arrow is the notion of I, of everything to which we are chained. The Buddha says that we shouldn't waste time on useless questions. Is the universe finite or infinite? Does the Buddha live after Nirvana or not? All this is useless. What matters is that we pull the arrow out. It is an exorcism, a law of salvation.

The Buddha says: "As the vast ocean has only one flavor, the flavor of salt, so the flavor of the Law is the flavor of salvation." His followers have lost themselves (or found too much) in metaphysical disquisitions. But that is not the goal of Buddhism. A Buddhist may profess any religion as long as he follows the Law. What is important is salvation and the four noble truths: suffering, the origin of suffering, the curing of suffering, and the way to arrive at the cure. At the end is Nirvana. The order of the truths doesn't matter. It has been said that they correspond to the traditional medical formulation of sickness, diagnosis, treatment, and cure. The cure, in this case, is Nirvana.

Now we come to the difficult part, which our Western minds tend to reject: transmigration, which for us is a poetic notion. What transmigrates is not the soul, because Buddhism denies the existence of a soul, but rather the karma, which is a sort of mental organism and which is transmigrated an infinite number of times. In the West the idea has been propounded by various thinkers, above all by Pythagoras—who recognized the shield with which he had fought in the Trojan War, when he had another name. In the tenth book of Plato's *Republic* is the dream of Er, a soldier who watches the souls choose their fates before drinking in the river of Oblivion. Agamemnon chooses to be an eagle, Orpheus a swan, and Odysseus—who once called himself Nobody—chooses to be the most modest, the most unknown of men.

There is a passage in Empedocles of Agrigentum where he recalls his previous lives: "I was a maiden, I was a branch, I was a deer, and I was a mute fish who leapt from the sea." Caesar attributes this doctrine to the Druids. The Welsh poet Taliesin says that there is not a single form in the universe he has not had: "I have been a leader in battle, I have been a sword in the hand, I have been a bridge that crossed sixty rivers, I was bewitched into sea foam, I have been a star, I have been a light, I have been a tree, I have been a word in a book, I have been a book in the beginning." There is a poem of Darío, perhaps his most beautiful, which begins like this: "I was a soldier who slept in the bed/ of Cleopatra the queen . . ."

Transmigration has been a great theme of literature. We also encounter it among the mystics. Plotinus says that to pass from one life to another is like sleeping in different beds in different rooms. I imagine all of us have had the sensation of having lived previous lives. In the beautiful poem by Dante Gabriel Rossetti, "Sudden Light," he says, "I have been here before." It is addressed to a woman whom he has possessed or will possess, and he tells her that she has already been his, and has been his an infinite number of times, and will be his forever. This takes us to the doctrine of cycles, which is close to Buddhism, and which St. Augustine refuted in *The City of God.*

News of the Hindu doctrine reached the Stoics and Pythagoreans: the idea that the universe consists of an infinite number of cycles, divided into kalpas. The kalpa transcends the imagination of man. Think of a wall of iron. It is sixteen miles high, and every six hundred years an angel brushes against it with a fine cloth from Benares. When the cloth has worn down that sixteen-mile-high iron wall, the first day of a kalpa will have passed. The gods last for as long as a kalpa, and then they too die and are reborn.

The history of the universe is divided into cycles, and within these cycles there are great eclipses in which nothing or only the words of the Vedas remain. Those words are the archetypes that create things. The god Brahma also dies and is reborn. There is a somewhat pathetic moment in which Brahma is found in his palace. He has been reborn after one of the kalpas, after one of the eclipses. He walks through the rooms, which are empty. He thinks of the other gods. The other gods appear at his command; and they think that Brahma has created them because they were there before.

Let us pause for a moment in this vision of the history of the universe. In Buddhism there is no god; or there may be a god, but that is not what is essential. The essential is that we believe our destiny has been preordained by our karma. If I happen to have been born in Buenos Aires in 1899, if I happen to be blind, if I happen to be speaking these words before you tonight, all this is the result of my previous life. There is not a single fact of my life that has not been preordained by my previous life. This is what is called karma. Karma, as I have said, becomes a mental structure, a very delicate mental structure.

In every moment of our lives we are weaving and interweaving. What we weave is not only our will, our acts, our half-dreams, our sleep, our half-waking; we are forever weaving our karma. And when we die, another being will be born who is the heir of that karma.

Deussen—a disciple of Schopenhauer, who loved Buddhism so much—tells how in India he met a blind beggar and became friends with him. The beggar told him: "If I have been born blind, it is because of the sins committed in my previous life; it is just if I am blind." The people accept suffering. Gandhi opposed the building of hospitals. He said that hospitals and charitable works simply delay the paying of a debt. One being cannot help another: if the others suffer, then they must suffer, to pay for a sin. If I help them, then I am putting off their payment of this debt.

Karma is a cruel law, but it has a curious mathematical consequence: if my present life is determined by my previous life, that previous life was determined by another, and that by another, and so on forever. That is to say: the letter z is determined by y, y by x, x by w, w by v, except that this alphabet has an end but no beginning. The Buddhists and the Hindus, in general, believe in a living infinity. They believe that to arrive at this moment an infinite time has already passed. In saying infinite I do not mean indefinite, innumerable—I mean strictly *infinite*.

Among the six fates that are permitted for men—one can be a demon, a plant, an animal—the most difficult is to be a man, and we must make use of it in order to save ourselves.

The Buddha imagined that at the bottom of the sea is a tortoise and a floating bangle. Every six hundred years the tortoise sticks its head out. It would be extraordinary if it put its head through the bangle. But, said the Buddha, to be human is as rare as the tortoise putting its head through the bangle. Yet we must be men before we may reach Nirvana.

What is the cause of suffering, the cause of life, if we deny the concept of a god, if there is no personal deity who has created the universe? It is what the Buddha called zen. The word zen may seem strange, but we will compare it to other words we know.

Let us think, for example, of the *will* of Schopenhauer. Schopenhauer conceived of *Die Welt als Wille und Vorstellung*, the world as will and representation. There is a will embodied in each one of us, and it produces the representation that is the world. We find this in other philosophies under different names. Bergson speaks of the *élan vital*, Bernard Shaw of the *life force*, which is the same. But there is a difference: for Bergson and Shaw the *élan vital* is a force we impose—we keep dreaming the world, creating the world. For Schopenhauer, the somber Schopenhauer, and for the Buddha, the world is a dream. We must stop dreaming it, and we can only stop through great effort. We have the principle of suffering, which becomes zen. Zen produces life, and life is powerfully wretched. What does it mean to live? To live is to be born, grow old, grow sick, die—not to mention the other sorrows, including the one that was, for the Buddha, the most pathetic: not to be with those we love.

We must renounce passion. Suicide does not help, because it is a passionate act. The man who commits suicide remains in the world of dreams. We must reach the understanding that the world is an apparition, a dream; that life is a dream. But we must feel this deeply, having reached it through the exercises of meditation. In the Buddhist monasteries one of the exercises is this: the neophyte must live every moment of his life experiencing it fully. He must think: "Now it is noon; now I am crossing the patio; now I will meet the superior." And at the same time he must think that the noon, the patio, and the superior are unreal, that they are as unreal as he and his thoughts, for Buddhism denies the I.

One of the great delusions is the I. Buddhism thus agrees with Hume, with Schopenhauer, and with our own Macedonio Fernández. There is no subject; what exists is a series of mental states. If I say "I think," I am committing an error, because I am assuming a fixed subject and then an act of that subject, which is thought. It is not so. One should say, as Hume points out, not "I think," but rather "it is thought," as one says "it is raining." When we say "it is raining," we do not think that the rain is performing an act but rather that something is *happening*. In the same way that we say "it's hot," "it's cold," we should also say "it's thinking," "it's suffering," and avoid the subject.

In the monasteries the neophytes are subjected to a rigorous discipline. Anyone may leave the monastery at any time. They do not even note, I've been told, anyone's name. The neophyte enters the monastery, and they subject him to harsh labors. He sleeps, and after a quarter of an hour they wake him; he must clean and sweep; if he falls asleep they physically punish him. Thus he must continually think, not on his sins, but on the unreality of everything. He must perform a continuous exercise of unreality.

We now come to Zen Buddhism and to Bodhidharma, the great missionary. In the fifth century A.D. Bodhidharma traveled from India to China. There he met an emperor who fostered Buddhism. The emperor enumerated the monasteries and shrines he had built and the many neophytes studying within them. Bodhidharma said to him: "All of this belongs to the world of illusion. The monasteries and monks are as unreal as you and I." Then he went to meditate and sat against a wall.

The teaching reached Japan and split into various sects, the most famous of which is Zen. In Zen they have discovered a procedure to reach illumination. It only works after years of meditation. It arrives suddenly: it is not the product of a series of syllogisms. One must suddenly intuit the truth. The process is called satori, and it consists of a sudden event that is beyond logic.

We always think in terms of subject-object, cause-effect, logic-illogic, a thing and its opposite. We must go beyond these categories. According to the Zen masters, to reach truth through sudden intuition requires an illogical answer. The neophyte asks the teacher, "What is the Buddha?" The teacher answers: "The cypress is the orchard." An answer which is completely illogical but which may awaken the truth. The neophyte asks why Bodhidharma came from the West. The teacher replies: "Three pounds of linen." These words do not contain an allegorical meaning; they are a nonsensical answer to awaken, suddenly, the intuition. It may also be a sudden blow. The disciple may ask something, and the teacher may answer with a slap. There is a story—though it must be legendary—about Bodhidharma.

Bodhidharma was accompanied by a disciple who kept asking questions, and Bodhidharma never answered. The disciple attempted to meditate, and after a while he cut off his left arm and presented it to the master as proof that he wanted to be his disciple. The master, without paying any attention to the gift—because in the end everything is a physical matter, an illusory matter—asked him, "What do you want?" The disciple replied: "I have been looking for my mind for a long time, and I haven't found it." The master said: "You have not found it because it doesn't exist." At that moment the disciple understood the truth, understood that the I does not exist, understood that everything is unreal. Here we have, more or less, the essence of Zen Buddhism.

It is very difficult to explicate a religion, particularly a religion one does not profess. I think that what is important in Buddhism is not its diverting legends but its discipline: a discipline that is within our reach and does not require us to become ascetics. Nor does it ask us to abandon the carnal life. What it requires is meditation, and meditation that has nothing to do with our sins, with our past lives.

One of the subjects of Zen Buddhist meditation is to think that your past life is illusory. If I were a Buddhist monk, I would be thinking at this very moment that I had just begun to live, that all the earlier life of Borges was a dream, that all of universal history is a dream. Through exercises of an intellectual kind we will become free of zen. Once we understand that the I does not exist, we will not think that the I can be happy or that our task is to make it happy. We will reach a state of calm. This is not to say that Nirvana is equivalent to a cessation of thinking. A proof of it is in the legend of the Buddha. The Buddha, beneath his sacred pipal tree, reached Nirvana, and yet he continued to live and teach the law for many years.

What does it mean to reach Nirvana? Simply that our acts no longer cast shadows. While we are in this world we are subject to karma. Every one of our acts is interwoven into this mental structure called karma. When we have reached Nirvana our acts no longer have shadows; we are free. St. Augustine said that when we are saved we will have no reason to think about good or evil. We will continue to do good, without thinking of it.

What is Nirvana? A large part of the attention that Buddhism has gained in the West is due to that beautiful word. It seems impossible it does not contain something precious. Nirvana is, literally, extinction, extinguishing. It is conjectured that when one reaches Nirvana he is extinguished. But when one dies there is a great Nirvana, and then extinction. However, an Austrian Orientalist has noted that the Buddha employed the physics of his time, and the idea of extinction was not the same as it is today. It was thought that a flame, when extinguished, did not disappear. It kept living, it endured in another state. Therefore Nirvana does not mean extinction, it means that we continue in another way, in a way that is inconceivable for us. In general, the metaphors of the mystics are nuptial; those of the Buddhists are different. When one speaks of Nirvana, one does not speak of the wine of Nirvana or the rose of Nirvana or the embrace of Nirvana. One compares it to an island, an unmoving island surrounded by torments. It is compared to a tower or to a garden. It is something which exists on its own, beyond us.

What I have said tonight is fragmentary. It would have been absurd if I had expounded a doctrine to which I have dedicated some years—and of which I have actually understood little—with the intention of displaying a museum piece. Buddhism is not a museum piece; it is a path to salvation. Not for me, but for millions of men. I hope that I have treated it with respect, discussing it here tonight.

Poetry

THE IRISH PANTHEIST Scotus Erigena said that the Holy Scripture contains an infinite number of meanings, and he compared it to the iridescent feathers of a peacock's tail. Centuries later, a Spanish Kabbalist said that God wrote the Scriptures for each one of the men of Israel, that there are as many Bibles as there are readers of the Bible. This is believable if we consider that the author of the Bible and the author of the destiny of each one of its readers is the same. One may think of these two sentences merely as demonstrations of the Celtic imagination and of the Oriental imagination. But I would venture to say that they are both absolutely correct, not only in regard to the Scriptures but to any book worth rereading.

Emerson said that a library is a magic chamber in which there are many enchanted spirits. They wake when we call them. When the book lies unopened, it is literally, geometrically, a volume, a thing among things. When we open it, when the book surrenders itself to its reader, the aesthetic event occurs. And even for the same reader the same book changes, for we change; we are the river of Heraclitus, who said that the man of yesterday is not the man of today, who will not be the man of tomorrow. We change incessantly, and each reading of a book, each rereading, each memory of that rereading, reinvents the text. The text too is the changing river of Heraclitus.

This brings us to the doctrine of Croce, who may not be the most profound thinker but is the least prejudiced: the idea that literature is expression. From that comes Croce's other doctrine, one which is frequently forgotten: if literature is expression, literature is made of words, and language is also an aesthetic phenomenon. That is something difficult for us to admit: the concept that language is an aesthetic event. Almost no one professes Croce's doctrine yet everyone applies it continually.

We say that Spanish is a sonorous language, that English is a language of varied sounds, that Latin has a certain dignity to which all the later languages aspired: we apply aesthetic categories to languages. Erroneously we suppose that language corresponds to that mysterious thing we call reality. The truth is that language is something else.

Let us imagine something yellow, shining, changing. That thing is something in the sky, circular; at other times it has the form of an arc, other times it grows and shrinks. Someone—we will never know the name of that someone— our ancestor, our common ancestor, gives to that thing the name *moon*, different in different languages and variously lovely. I would say that the Greek word *selene* is too complex for the moon, that the English *moon* has something slow, something that imposes on the voice a slowness that suits the moon, that seems like the moon because it is almost circular: it begins almost with the same letter with which it ends. As for the Spanish *luna*, that beautiful word we inherited from the Latin and share with the Italian: it consists of two syllables, two pieces, which are perhaps too much. We have *lua* in Portuguese, which seems less lovely; and *lune* in French, which has something mysterious. In German, the word for moon is masculine. Thus Nietzsche could say that the moon is a monk who gazes enviously at the earth, or a cat, *Kater*, who walks on rugs of stars.

We imagine that someone, somewhere, invented the word *moon*. No doubt that first invention was something quite different. But why didn't it end with that first person who named the moon with that sound or another?

There is a Persian metaphor which says that the moon is the mirror of time. In that phrase, *mirror of time*, is the fragility of the moon and also its eternity. It is the contradiction of the moon, so nearly translucid, so nearly nothing, but whose measure is eternity. To say *moon* or to say *mirror of time* are two aesthetic events, except that the latter is the work of a second stage, because *mirror of time* is composed of two unities, while *moon* gives us, perhaps more effectively, the word, the concept of the moon. Each word is a poetic work.

It is said that prose is closer to reality than poetry. I think this is wrong. There is an idea that has been attributed to the short story writer Horacio Quiroga: if a cold wind blows from the bank of the river, one must write simply, "a cold wind blows from the bank of the river." Quiroga—if it was he who said this—seems to have forgotten that that construction is as far from reality as it is from the cold wind that blows from the bank of the river. What is our perception of it? We feel the air move, we call it *wind*; we feel that that wind comes from a certain direction, from the bank of the river. And with this we form something as complex as a poem by Góngora or a sentence by Joyce. Let us return to that phrase, "a cold wind blows from the bank of the river." We create a subject, *wind*, a verb, *blows*, and a context, *from the bank of the river*. All of this is far from reality. Reality is something simpler. That apparently prosaic and ordinary line, deliberately chosen as such by Quiroga, is a complicated phrase; it is a structure.

Let us take Carducci's famous line: "The green silence of the fields." We might think that this is a mistake, that Carducci has misplaced the adjective; that he meant to write "The silence of the green fields." Astutely or rhetorically, he altered it and spoke of the green silence of the fields. How do we perceive it? We feel various things at the same time. (The word *thing* is perhaps too substantive.) We feel the field, the vast presence of the field, we feel the verdure and the silence. The fact that there is a word for silence is an aesthetic creation. *Silence* applied to people. To apply it to the circumstance that there was no sound in the field is an aesthetic operation, one that no doubt was bold in its time. When Carducci says, "The green silence of the fields," he is saying something that is as near and as far from immediate reality as if he had said, "The silence of the green fields."

We have another famous example of hypallage, that unsurpassed line of Virgil, "*Ibant obscuri sola sub nocte per umbram*," "They went darkly beneath the solitary night through the shadows." We may leave aside the *per umbram*, which rounds out the line, and take "They [Aeneas and the Sybil] went darkly beneath the solitary night." (*Solitary* has more force in Latin because it comes before *sub*.) We might think that Virgil had switched words, because the natural thing to say would have been, "They went alone beneath the dark night." Nevertheless, in trying to recreate the image, we think of Aeneas and the Sybil, and we see that it is as close to our image to say, "They went darkly beneath the solitary night," as it is to say, "They went alone beneath the dark night."

Language is an aesthetic creation. I think there is no

question of that. A proof is that when we study a language, when we are obliged to see the words up close, we experience them as beautiful or not. Studying a language, one sees the words with a magnifying glass; one thinks, this word is ugly, this lovely, this too heavy. This does not happen in one's mother tongue, where the words do not appear to us isolated from speech.

Poetry, said Croce, is expression, if a line is expression, if each one of the parts from which the verse is made, each one of the words, is in itself expressive. You will say that this is trite, something that everybody knows. But I don't know if we know it; I think we feel it because it is true.

The fact is that poetry is not the books in the library, not the books in Emerson's magic chamber. Poetry is the encounter of the reader with the book, the discovery of the book.

There is another aesthetic experience, also quite strange —the one in which the poet conceives the work, in which he is discovering or inventing the work. As is well known, in Latin the word for *to invent* and *to discover* is the same. All of this is in accord with the Platonic doctrine that to invent, to discover, is to remember. Francis Bacon agreed that learning is remembering, not knowing is knowing to forget; everything is this way, only we don't see it.

When I write something, I have the sensation that it existed before. I start from a general conception. I know more or less the beginning and the end, and then I discover the intervening parts. But I do not have the sensation of having invented them, that they depend on my free will. The things are as they are, but they are hidden, and my task as a poet is to find them.

Bradley said that one of the effects of poetry is that it gives us the impression not of discovering something new but of remembering something we have forgotten. When we read a good poem we imagine that we too could have written it; that the poem already existed within us. This brings us to the Platonic definition of poetry: that winged, fickle, sacred thing. As a definition it is fallible, since that winged, fickle, sacred thing could also be music (except that poetry is a form of music). Plato, defining poetry, gives us an example of poetry. And this brings us to the idea that poetry is an aesthetic experience: something that would be a revolution in the teaching of poetry.

I have been a professor of English literature in the College of Philosophy and Letters at the University of Buenos Aires, and I have tried to disregard as much as possible the history of literature. When my students asked me for a bibliography, I told them, "A bibliography is unimportant—after all, Shakespeare knew nothing of Shakespearean criticism. Why not study the texts directly? If you like the book, fine; if you don't, don't read it. The idea of compulsory reading is absurd; it's only worthwhile to speak of compulsory happiness. I believe that poetry is something one feels. If you don't feel poetry, if you have no sense of beauty, if a story doesn't make you want to know what happened next, then the author has not written for you. Put it aside. Literature is rich enough to offer you some other author worthy of your attention—or one today unworthy of your attention whom you will read tomorrow."

This is how I have taught, relying on the aesthetic event, which does not need to be defined. The aesthetic event is something as evident, as immediate, as indefinable as love, the taste of fruit, of water. We feel poetry as we feel the closeness of a woman, or as we feel a mountain or a bay. If we feel it immediately, why dilute it with other words, which no doubt will be weaker than our feelings?

There are people who barely feel poetry, and they are generally dedicated to teaching it. I believe in feeling poetry and not in having it taught. I have not taught the love of particular texts; I have taught my students how to love literature, how to see literature as a form of happiness. I am almost incapable of abstract thought—you will have noticed that I'm continually propping myself up with quotations and memories. Rather than speaking abstractly of poetry, which is a form of ennui or of loafing, let us take two Spanish poems and examine them.

I choose two well-known poems because my memory is fallible, and I prefer a text that already exists in your memories. We will consider the famous sonnet of Quevedo, written to the memory of Don Pedro Téllez Girón, Duke of Osuna. I will recite it slowly, and then we will go back to it, line by line.

> *Faltar pudo su patria al grande Osuna,*
> *pero no a su defensa sus hazañas;*
> *diéronle muerte y cárcel las Españas,*
> *de quien él hizo esclava la Fortuna.*
>
> *Lloraron sus invidias una a una*
> *con las proprias naciones las extrañas;*
> *su tumba son de Flandres las campañas,*
> *y su epitafio la sangrienta Luna.*
>
> *En sus exequias encendio al Vesubio*
> *Parténope y Trinacria al Mongibelo;*
> *el llanto militar crecio en diluvio.*
>
> *Dióle el mejor lugar Marte en su cielo;*
> *la Mosa, el Rhin, el Tajo, y el Danubio*
> *murmuran con dolor su desconsuelo.*

[The great Osuna might lack his homeland,| but
not the deeds in its defense;| Spain brought
death and jail| to him whom Fortune made a
slave.|| They wept in envy, one by one,| foreign
nations and his own;| his tomb is the campaigns
of Flanders,| and his epitaph the bloody moon.||
For his obsequies Parthenope| lit Vesuvius, and
Trinacria the Mongibelo;| the military weeping
grew into a flood.|| Mars gave him the best
place in heaven;| the Moselle, the Rhine, the
Tagus, and the Danube | in sorrow murmur their
grief.]

The first thing I want to observe is that it deals with a
juridical allegation. The poet wants to defend the memory
of the Duke of Osuna who, as he wrote in another poem,
"died in prison and dead was a prisoner." The poet says that
Spain owes the duke great military honors, but they have
repaid him with jail. This lacks total validity, as there is no
reason why a hero couldn't be guilty or why a hero shouldn't
by punished. Nevertheless,

> *Faltar pudo su patria al grande Osuna,*
> *pero no a su defensa sus hazañas;*
> *diéronle muerte y cárcel las Españas,*
> *de quien él hizo esclava la Fortuna.*

is a demogogical moment. I am not speaking for or against
the sonnet; I am trying to analyze it.

> *Lloraron sus invidias una a una*
> *con las proprias naciones las extrañas;*

These two lines do not have major poetic resonance; they are placed there by the necessity of elaborating a sonnet. Quevedo followed the difficult form of the Italian sonnet, which required four rhymes. Shakespeare followed the easy form of the Elizabethan sonnet, which required two. Quevedo continues:

> *su tumba son de Flandres las campañas,*
> *y su epitafio la sangrienta Luna.*

Here is the essential. Those two lines owe their richness to ambiguity. I remember many discussions on the interpretation of those lines. What does it mean that "his tomb was the campaigns of Flanders"? We may think of the fields of Flanders, of the military campaigns the duke waged. "And his epitaph the bloody moon" is one of the most memorable lines in the Spanish language. What does it mean? We think of the bloody moon that figures in the Apocalypse, or of the moon properly red over the field of battle. But there is another sonnet of Quevedo, also dedicated to the Duke of Osuna, where he says, "to the moons of Thrace with bloody/ eclipse your journey now is sealed." Quevedo would have thought first of the Ottoman flag: the bloody moon would be the red half-moon. I think we are all agreed that none of the meanings should be discarded. We will not say that Quevedo is referring only to military travels, or to the duke's services, or to the campaign of Flanders, or to the bloody moon over the battlefield, or to the Turkish flag. Quevedo perceived the various meanings. The lines are good because they are ambiguous.

> *En sus exequias encendio al Vesubio*
> *Parténope y Trinacria al Mongibelo;*

That is to say that Naples has lit Vesuvius, and Sicily Etna. How strange that these ancient names have been placed here—they seem so remote from the illustrious names that came later.

> *el llanto militar crecio en diluvio.*

Here we have another proof that poetry is one thing and rational feeling another: the image of soldiers who weep until they produce a deluge is notoriously absurd. But it is not absurd in poetry, which has its own laws. The "military weeping"—the word "military"—is surprising. "Military" is an astonishing adjective when applied to weeping.

> *Dióle el mejor lugar Marte en su cielo;*

Nor can we logically justify this: it makes no sense to think that Mars will quarter the Duke of Osuna next to Caesar. The phrase exists by virtue of the hyperbaton. It is the touchstone of poetry: the line exists beyond meaning.

> *la Mosa, el Rhin, el Tajo y el Danubio*
> *murmuran con dolor su desconsuelo.*

I would say that these lines which have moved me for years are, nonetheless, basically false. Quevedo allowed himself to be dragged along by the idea of a hero wept over by the geography of his campaigns and by famous rivers. We feel that it is false: it would have been better to tell the truth, to say what Wordsworth said, for example, at the end of that sonnet in which he attacks Douglas for having felled a forest. He says, yes, it was terrible what Douglas did to the forest, destroying a noble horde, "a brotherhood of venerable Trees." And yet, he adds, we suffer the pains of evils which do not matter to nature—the river Tweed and the green pastures and the hills and the mountains continue regardless. He felt he could have a greater effect by speaking the truth. It pains us that they have destroyed those beautiful trees, but to nature it doesn't matter. Nature—if there exists an entity called Nature—knows that it can restore them. The river keeps flowing.

It is true that for Quevedo it is a matter of the gods of those rivers. Perhaps it would have been more poetic had he written that the death of the Duke of Osuna doesn't concern the rivers at all. But Quevedo wanted to create an elegy, a poem on the death of a man. What is the death of a man? With him dies a face that will not occur again, as Pliny observed. Each man has his own unique face, and with him die thousands of events, thousands of memories, all of them too human. Quevedo seems to feel none of this. His friend, the Duke of Osuna, has died in jail, and Quevedo writes this sonnet with coldness; we feel its essential indifference. He writes it as an allegation against the state which condemned the duke to prison. It might even seem that he didn't like the duke. And yet, it is one of the great sonnets of our language.

We will go on to another sonnet, one by Enrique Banchs. It would be absurd to say that Banchs is a better poet than Quevedo. Besides, what do such comparisons mean? Let us consider this sonnet by Banchs and see what makes it so pleasurable.

> *Hospitalario y fiel en su reflejo*
> *donde a ser apariencia se acostumbra*
> *el material vivir, está el espejo*
> *como un claro de luna en la penumbra.*

Pompa le da en las noches la flotante
claridad de la lámpara, y tristeza
la rosa que en el vaso agonizante
también en él inclina la cabeza.

Si hace doble al dolor, también repite
las cosas que me son jardín del alma.
Y acaso espera que algún día habite

en la ilusión de su azulada calma
el Huésped que le deje reflejadas
frentes juntas y manos enlazadas.

[Hospitable and faithful in its reflection| where
living matter is accustomed| to being
appearance, the mirror is| like moonlight in the
darkness.|| Pomp it brings to the nights the
floating| clarity of a lamp, and sadness| the
rose that in the vase dying| leans its head
within it too.|| If it doubles pain, it also
repeats| the things which for me are a garden
of the soul.| And perhaps it hopes that some
day will live|| in the illusion of its blue calm|
the Guest who will leave reflected| foreheads
joined and hands interlaced.]

This sonnet is quite curious, because the mirror is not
the protagonist: there is a secret protagonist who is revealed
to us at the end. First of all we have the theme, which is so
poetic: the mirror that duplicates the appearance of all
things.

We may remember Plotinus. They wanted to paint his
portrait, and he refused, saying "I myself am a shadow, a
shadow of the archetype that is in the sky. What is the point

of making a shadow of that shadow?" What is art, thought Plotinus, but an apparition of the second degree? If man is frail, how can an image of a man be loved? This is what Banchs felt. He felt the phantasmic quality of the mirror.

It is truly awful that there are mirrors; I have always been terrified by mirrors. I think that Poe felt it too. There is an essay of his, one of the least known, on the decoration of rooms. One of the conditions he insists on is that the mirrors be placed in such a way that a seated person is not reflected. This tells us his fear of seeing himself in the mirror. We see it in his story "William Wilson" about the double, and also in *The Narrative of Arthur Gordon Pym*, where there is an Antarctic tribe, and a man from that tribe sees a mirror for the first time and collapses, horrified. We are accustomed to mirrors, but there is something terrifying in that visual duplication of reality.

Let us return to the sonnet by Banchs. "Hospitable" gives it a human touch. Nevertheless, we have never thought of mirrors as hospitable. Mirrors are received in silence, with amiable resignation.

> *Hospitalario y fiel en su reflejo*
> *donde a ser apariencia se acostumbra*
> *el material vivir, está el espejo*
> *como un claro de luna en la penumbra.*

We see the mirror, itself luminous, and he also compares it to something as intangible as the moon. He continues to feel the magic and strangeness of the mirror: "like moon-light on shadow."

> *Pompa le da en las noches la flotante*
> *claridad de la lámpara . . .*

The "floating clarity" means that things cannot be defined; everything must be imprecise like the mirror, the mirror of shadow. It is probably late afternoon or night.

> . . . *la flotante*
> *claridad de la lámpara, y tristeza*
> *la rosa que en el vaso agonizante*
> *también en él inclina la cabeza.*

So that everything will not be vague, we now have a rose, a precise rose.

> *Si hace doble al dolor, también repite*
> *las cosas que me son jardin del alma.*
> *Y acaso espera que algún dia habite*
>
> *en la ilusión de su azulada calma,*
> *el Huésped que le deje reflejadas*
> *frentes juntas y manos enlazadas.*

Here we reach the subject of the sonnet, which is not the mirror but love, modest love. The mirror does not hope to see reflected foreheads joined and hands enlaced, it is the poet who hopes to see them. But a sort of modesty brings him to say all this in an indirect manner. This is admirably prepared: from the beginning we have "hospitable and faithful"; from the beginning the mirror is not a mirror of glass or of metal. The mirror is a human being; it is hospitable and faithful and then it accustoms us to see the world of appearances, a world that is finally identified with the poet. The poet is he who hopes to see the Guest, love.

I have spoken of languages and of how unfair it is to compare one with another. If we think of a poem, a stanza in Spanish, for example:

> *quién hubiera tal ventura*
> *sobre las aguas del mar*
> *como hubo el conde Arnaldos*
> *la mañana de San Juan*

[who had such luck| on the waters of the sea| as
had the Count Arnaldos| the morning of San
Juan]

The Count Arnaldos or the morning of San Juan do not
matter: those lines could only be said in Spanish.

The sound of French I don't find particularly agreeable.
I think it lacks the sonority of other Latin tongues. But how
can one think badly of a language which allows lines as
marvelous as this one by Hugo:

> *L'hydre-Univers tordant son corps écaillé d'astres*

How can we condemn a language without which those lines
would be impossible?

As for English, I think it has the defect of having lost
the open vowels of Old English. Nevertheless, it offered the
possibility to Shakespeare of lines like:

> *And shake the yoke of inauspicious stars*
> *From this world-wearied flesh*

If I had to choose a language—though there is no
reason for not choosing any one of them—for me that
language would be German, which has the possibility of
forming compound words (like English, but more so), has
open vowels and a fine music. As for Italian, the *Commedia*
is enough.

Nothing is more wonderful than the fact of so much beauty dispersed among the various languages. My teacher, the great Spanish Jewish poet Rafael Cansinos-Asséns, left us a prayer to the Lord in which he says, "O Lord, let there not be so much beauty." Browning wrote that

> *Just when we're safest, there's a sunset-touch,*
> *A fancy from a flower bell, someone's death,*
> *A chorus-ending from Euripides—*

and we are again lost.

Beauty waits in ambush for us. If we are sensitive, we will feel it in the poetry of all languages.

I ought to have studied the Oriental languages: I have only glanced at them through translations. But I have felt the punch, the impact of their beauty. For example, that line by the Persian poet Hafiz: "I fly, my dust will be what I am." In this there is the whole doctrine of transmigration. "My dust will be what I am." I will be reborn again and again; in another country, I will be Hafiz, the poet. All of this is given in a few words which I have read in English, but which cannot be very different in Persian. It is too simple to have been altered greatly.

Beauty is everywhere, perhaps in every moment of our lives. My friend Roy Bartholomew, who lived for some years in Persia and translated Omar Khayyam directly from the Farsi, has told me what I already guessed: that in the East, in general, they do not read literature and philosophy historically. They study the history of philosophy as though Aristotle were disputing with Bergson, Plato with Hume, all at the same time. This greatly disturbed Deussen and Max Müller, who could not determine the chronology of the authors they were studying.

I will end by citing three prayers by Phoenician sailors, from the first century. These prayers were spoken when the ship was on the verge of being lost. The first is:

Mother of Carthage, I return my oar.

Mother of Carthage is the city of Tyre, where Dido came from. And then, "I return my oar." There is something extraordinary here: the Phoenician can only conceive of life as an oarsman. He has completed his life, and he gives back his oar so that others may continue to row.

Another of the prayers, one even more pathetic:

I sleep; presently I row again.

The man does not conceive of any other fate. It also shows the idea of cyclical time.

Finally, this one, which is quite disturbing and is different from the others, because it does not imply an acceptance of fate. It is the despair of a man who is going to die, who is going to be judged by terrible gods, and says:

Gods, judge me not as a God
but as a man
whom the Ocean has broken.

In these three prayers we immediately feel—or at least I do—the presence of poetry. Here is the aesthetic event, not in the libraries or the bibliographies or the studies of chronologies of manuscripts or the closed volumes.

I read those three prayers of Phoenician sailors in a story by Kipling, "The Manner of Men," a story about St.

Paul. Are they authentic (as they say) or were they written by Kipling, the great poet? After formulating the question I felt guilty, because what is the point in choosing? Let us look at the two possibilities, the two horns of the dilemma.

In the first case, we are dealing with the prayers of Phoenician sailors, people of the sea who could only conceive of life on the sea. From Phoenician, let us say, they passed to Greek, from Greek to Latin, from Latin to English. Kipling rewrote them.

In the second case, a great poet, Rudyard Kipling, imagines the Phoenician sailors: in some way he is close to them, in some way he *is* them. He conceives of life as a life on the sea, and he puts these prayers in their mouths. Everything happened in the past: the anonymous Phoenician sailors are dead, Kipling is dead. What does it matter which of these ghosts wrote or thought these lines?

There is an odd metaphor in a Hindu poem, one which I am not sure I can completely appreciate. It says that the Himalayas—those high mountains whose peaks are, according to Kipling, the knees of other mountains—the Himalayas are the smile of Shiva. The high mountains are the smile of a god, a terrible god. It is a startling metaphor.

For me, beauty is a physical sensation, something we feel with our whole body. It is not the result of a judgment. We do not arrive at it by way of rules. We either feel beauty or we don't.

I will end with a great line by the poet who, in the seventeenth century, took the strangely real and poetic name of Angelus Silesius. It is the summary of all I have said tonight—except that I have said it by means of reasoning and simulated reasoning. I will say it first in Spanish and then in German:

La rosa sin porqué florece porque florece.

Die Rose ist ohne warum; sie blühet weil sie blühet.

[The rose has no why, it flowers because it flowers.]

✥ The Kabbalah ✥

THE DIVERSE, AND occasionally contradictory, teachings grouped under the name of the Kabbalah derive from a concept alien to the Western mind, that of the sacred book. We have an analogous concept—the classic book—but I think it is easy to demonstrate, with the help of Oswald Spengler and his book *Der Untergang des Abendlandes* (*The Decline of the West*), that the two concepts are quite different.

Let us take the word *classic*. What does it mean, etymologically? *Classic* comes from *classis*: a frigate, a fleet. A classic book is a well-run book; everything must be on board it—*shipshape* as they say in English. Besides this relatively modest sentiment, a classic book is one that is eminent in its genre. Thus we say that *Don Quixote*, the *Commedia*, and *Faust* are classics.

Although the cult of those books has been carried to extremes that are perhaps excessive, they are not sacred texts. The Greeks considered the *Iliad* and the *Odyssey* to be classic works. Alexander, as Plutarch tells us, kept under his pillow a copy of the *Iliad* and his sword, the two symbols of his destiny as a warrior. But it never occurred to the Greeks that the *Iliad* was perfect word for word. In Alexandria, the librarians gathered to study the *Iliad* and, in the course of those studies, they invented the indispensable (though at times now disgracefully forgotten) punctuation marks. The *Iliad* was an eminent book; it was considered the apex of poetry. But it was not thought that every word, every hexameter was inevitably admirable. It was seen as something changeable, and it was studied in historical fashion; it was placed within a context. The concept of a sacred book is something entirely different. Horace said, "At times, good Homer nodded." No one would say that, at times, the good Holy Spirit nodded.

Today we think of a book as an instrument for justifying, defending, disputing, explicating, or chronicling a doctrine, but in Antiquity a book was seen only as a substitute for the spoken word. Let us remember the passage in Plato where he says that books are like statues: they may seem alive, but when you ask them something they do not reply. To overcome this difficulty, he invented the Platonic dialogue, which explores all of the possibilities of a subject.

We also have the lovely and curious letter that, according to Plutarch, Alexander of Macedon sent to Aristotle. He had just published his *Metaphysics*—that is, he had ordered various copies to be made. Alexander rebuked him, saying that now everyone could know what was previously known only to the elect. Aristotle responded in his own defense, no doubt with sincerity: "My treatise has been published and not published." He did not believe that a book expounded a subject completely, but rather that it served as a sort of guide to accompany oral instruction.

Pythagoras did not leave a single written line. It is conjectured that he did not want to tie himself to a text. He hoped that his thought would continue, after his death, to live and to branch out in the minds of his disciples. From that arises the phrase *magister dixit*, which is always misused. *Magister dixit* does not mean "the master has said it"—as a way to close off discussion. A Pythagorean proclaims a doctrine which is perhaps not in the tradition of Pythagoras, for example the doctrine of cyclical time. If it is attacked—"that is not in the tradition"—the response is *magister dixit*, which allows him to innovate. Pythagoras believed that books enchain, or, in the words of the Scriptures, that the letter kills and the spirit brings life.

Spengler points out in his chapter on magical culture in *Der Untergang des Abendlandes* that the prototype of the magical book is the Koran. For the ulema, the doctors of Moslem law, the Koran is not a book like the others. It is a book—this is incredible, but this is how it is—that is older than the Arabic language. One may not study it historically or philologically, because it is older than the Arabs, older than the language in which it exists, and older than the universe. Nor do they admit that the Koran is the work of God; it is something more intimate and mysterious. For the orthodox Moslems the Koran is an attribute of God, like His rage, His pity, or His justice. The Koran itself speaks of a mysterious book, the mother of the book, the celestial archetype of the Koran. It is in heaven and is worshiped by the angels.

Thus the notion of a sacred book is completely different from that of a classic book. In a sacred book, not only the words but the letters with which the words are written are sacred. The Kabbalists applied this concept to the study of the Scriptures. I suspect that their modus operandi was indebted to a desire to incorporate Gnostic thought into Jewish mysticism, to justify it with Scripture, to be orthodox. In any case, we may see briefly—I have almost no right to be discussing this—what is or what was the modus operandi of the Kabbalists, who began to apply their strange science in the south of France, in the north of Spain, in Catalonia, and then in Italy, Germany, and, to some extent, in other areas. They also reached Palestine, though it did not originate there: it came from the Gnostic and Catharist thinkers.

The idea is this: the Pentateuch, the Torah, is a sacred book. An infinite intelligence has condescended to the human task of producing a book. The Holy Spirit has condescended to literature, which is as incredible as imagining that God condescended to become a man. In that book, nothing can be accidental. (In human writing there is always something accidental.)

There is a superstitious veneration surrounding *Don Quixote*, *Macbeth*, or the *Chanson de Roland*, as there is for other books, generally one to a country. (Except in France, whose literature is so rich that it admits at least two classical traditions.) Well then—if a Cervantes scholar were to say: *Don Quixote* begins with two monosyllabic words ending in *n* (*en* and *un*), followed by one word of five letters (*lugar*), two of two letters (*de la*), and one of six (*Mancha*); and if he then were to draw conclusions from that, we would immediately assume he was mad. The Bible has been studied in this fashion.

It is said, for example, that it begins with the letter *bet*, the first letter of the first word, *b'reshit*. Why does it begin with *bet*? Because that is the first letter of the Hebrew word *b'rachah*, which means *blessing*. The text must begin with a blessing; it could not possibly begin with a letter that corresponds to a curse.

There is another circumstance, a curious one, which must have influenced the Kabbalah: God, whose words were the instrument of his work (as the great writer Saavedra Fajardo said) created the world through words: God said, Let there be light, and there was light. From this one came to the conclusion that light was created by the word *light*, or by the intonation with which God pronounced the word *light*. If He had said another word, or if he had pronounced the word in another way, the result might not have been light, but something else.

We now come to something as incredible as anything I've said so far. To something that must shock our Western minds—it shocks mine—but to which I must refer. When we think of words, we think historically: that words were first spoken and then later they became composed of letters. In contrast, the Kabbalah (which means *reception, tradition*) believes that the letters came first, that they were the instruments of God, not the words signified by the letters. It is as if one were to think of writing, contrary to experience, as older than the speaking of the language. Nothing, then, can be accidental in the Scriptures; everything must be pre-determined, including, for example, the number of letters in each verse.

They invented equivalences for the letters. They treated the Scriptures as if it were a coded writing, a cryptogram, and they deivised various rules for deciphering it. One may, for example, take each letter of each word and read it as the first letter of another word, thereby revealing a hidden text.

They also formed two alphabets: one, let us say, of *a* to *l* and the other of *m* to *z*. They took the letters above to be equivalent to those below. They also read the text—to use the Greek word—*boustrephedon*, that is, from right to left, then left to right, then right to left. They attributed numerical values to the letters. All of this formed a cryptography which could be deciphered, and the results were worthy of consideration, because they had all been foreseen by the infinite intelligence of God. Thus they arrived, by means of this cryptography, by this operation so reminiscent of Poe's

"The Gold-Bug," at the teachings. (I suspect that the teachings are older than the modus operandi, that what happened with the Kabbalah is the same as what happened with the philosophy of Spinoza: the geometric order came later. I would imagine that the Kabbalists were influenced by the Gnostics and that, in order to link everything to the Hebrew tradition, they sought this strange system of deciphering letters.)

The cosmic system of the Kabbalah may be described like this: In the beginning there is a Being analogous to the God of Spinoza, except that the God of Spinoza is infinitely rich. The *en sof*, in contrast, is infinitely poor, for of that Being we cannot say that He exists, for if we say that He exists then we must also say that stars exist, men exist, ants exist. How can we put them all in the same category? No, that primordial Being does not exist. Nor can we say that He thinks, because thinking is a logical process, moving from a premise to a conclusion. Nor can we say that He wants, because to want something is to feel the lack of something. Nor that He works, because to work is to propose a goal and to labor toward it. Besides, if the *en sof* is infinite, how can He want something else? And what other thing could He create except another infinite Being which would become confused with Himself? However, since the creation of the world is unfortunately necessary, we have ten emanations, the Sefirot, which emerge from Him but come after Him.

The idea of an eternal Being which has always had these ten emanations is difficult to comprehend. These ten emanate one from the other. The text tells us that they correspond to the fingers of the hand. The first emanation is called the Crown, and it is comparable to a ray of light issuing from the *en sof*, a ray of light that does not diminish, an unlimited being which cannot be diminished. From the

Crown issues another emanation; from that, another; and from that, another—until there are ten. Each emanation is tripartite. One of the three parts communicates with the superior Being; the central part is the essence; and the third part communicates with the inferior Being.

The ten emanations form a man called Adam Kadmon, the Archetypal Man. That man is in heaven, and we are his reflection. Adam Kadmon, formed by the ten emanations, himself emanates a world, which emanates another, until there are four. The third is our material world, and the fourth is the infernal world. All of them are included in Adam Kadmon, who understands man and his microcosm: all things.

I am not dealing with a museum piece from the history of philosophy. I believe the system has an application: it can serve as a means of thinking, of trying to understand the universe. The Gnostics preceded the Kabbalists by many centuries. They had a similar system which postulated an indeterminate god. From that god called Pleroma (the Plenitude) emanates another god—I am following the perverse version of Irenaeus—and from that emanation another, and from that another. There is a tower of emanations, and each of them constitutes a heaven. There are three hundred and sixty-five in all, because astrology becomes mixed into it. When we reach the final emanation, where the divine part has been reduced to almost zero, we find the god called Jehovah, who created this world.

Why did He create this world so full of errors, so full of horror, so full of sins, so full of physical pain, so full of guilt, so full of crime? Because the Divinity had diminished itself until it reached Jehovah, who created this fallible world.

We have the same mechanism in the creations of the ten Sefirot and the four worlds. Those ten emanations, as they move farther from the *en sof*, from the limitless, from the hidden, from the *hidden ones* (as they are called in the figurative language of the Kabbalists), lose strength, until they reach the one who created this world, this world where we are, so exposed to misfortune, so momentary in its happiness. It is not an absurd idea. We are faced with an eternal problem, the problem of evil. It is treated splendidly in the Book of Job which, according to Froude, is the greatest work of literature.

You will recall the story of Job, the persecuted just man, the man who wants to justify himself before God, the man condemned by his friends. In the end God speaks to him from the whirlwind. He says that He is beyond human measure. He takes two curious examples, the elephant and the whale, and says that He created them. Max Brod observed that the elephant, Behemoth ("the animals") is so big its name is plural. Leviathan may be two monsters, the whale or the crocodile. God says that he is as incomprehensible as those monsters and may not be measured by man.

Spinoza comes to the same point when he says that to give human attributes to God is as if a triangle were to say that God is eminently triangular. To say that God is just or pitiful is as anthropomorphic as to claim that God has a face or eyes or hands.

We have, then, a superior Divinity and other, inferior emanations. Emanations seems to be the word least offensive, so that God is not blamed for the creation of this world. As Schopenhauer said, the blame lies with his ministers, not with the king.

There have been various defenses of evil. First, the classic defense of the theologians, who declare that evil is negative, that evil is simply the absence of good. For any sensible person this is obviously false. A physical pain is as vivid or more vivid than any pleasure. Misfortune is not the absence of fortune, it is something positive. When we are miserable, we feel it as misery.

Then there is the argument, elegant but quite false, of Leibniz. Imagine two libraries. The first is composed of a thousand copies of the *Aeneid*, which he assumes is a perfect book, as perhaps it is. The other contains a thousand books of various merit, and one of them is the *Aeneid*. Which of the two libraries is superior? Obviously the second. Leibniz comes to the conclusion that evil is necessary for the variety of the world. But he seems to forget that it is one thing that *there are* bad books in the library, and another thing *to be* those books. And if we are those books we are condemned to hell.

Not everyone has the ecstasy—and I don't know if he always had it—of Kierkegaard, who said that if there were one soul in hell necessary for the variety of the world, and if that soul were his, he would sing from the depths of hell the praises of the Almighty.

I don't know if it is easy to feel this. I don't know if, after a few minutes in hell, Kierkegaard would have continued to feel the same way. But the idea, as you see, refers to an essential problem, that of the existence of evil, which the Gnostics and the Kabbalists resolved in the same way.

They resolved it by declaring that the universe is the work of a deficient Divinity, one whose fraction of Divinity approaches zero, of a god who is not *the* God. Of a god who is a distant descendant of God. I don't know if our minds can function with words as vast and as vague as God or Divinity, or with Basilides' Gnostic doctrine of the three hundred and sixty-five emanations. But we can understand the idea of a deficient Divinity, one who must make this world out of shoddy materials. We come then to Bernard Shaw, who said "God is in the making." God is something that does not pertain to the past, and perhaps does not pertain to the future: it is Eternity. God is something that may be future. If we are magnanimous, if we are intelligent, if we are lucid, we will be helping to construct God.

In Wells's *The Undying Fire*, the plot follows that of the Book of Job, and its hero is similar. Under anaesthesia, the protagonist dreams that he enters a laboratory. The equipment is poor, and an old man is working there. The old man is God, and he is quite irritated. I'm doing what I can, he says, but it's a struggle dealing with this difficult material. For God, evil is the intractable material, and good the malleable. But good, in the long run, is destined to triumph and is triumphing. I don't know if you believe in progress. I do, at least in the form of Goethe's spiral: we advance and retreat, but ultimately we are improving. Perhaps intellectually we are also improving. A proof of it may be this humble event in which we take an interest in what the Kabbalists thought.

I would like to talk now about one of the myths, one of the most curious legends of the Kabbalah; the golem, which inspired the famous novel by Meyrink, which inspired a poem of mine. God takes a lump of earth (*Adam* means *red earth*), blows life into it, and creates Adam, who for the Kabbalists is the first golem. He has been created by the Divine word, by a breath of life. The Kabbalah says that all of the Pentateuch is the name of God, except that the letters are scrambled. Thus, if one possesses the name of God, or discovers the Tetragrammaton, the name of the four letters of God, and knows how to pronounce them correctly, one can create a world, and one can also create a golem, a man.

The legends of the golem have been beautifully explored by Gershom Scholem in his book *On the Kabbalah and Its Symbolism*, which I have just read. I think it is the clearest book on the subject. He has proven that it is almost useless to search for the original sources. I have also read the beautiful and, I think, accurate translation—I do not know Hebrew—by León Dujovne of the *Sefer Yetsirah*, the *Book of Creation*. These books were not written in order to teach the Kabbalah but to approach it; so that a student of the Kabbalah may read them and feel strengthened. But they do not tell all of the truth, like the treatises published and not published by Aristotle.

Let us return to the golem. It is believed that if a rabbi learns or happens to discover the secret name of God and pronounces it over a human figure made of clay, it will come to life and be a golem. In one of the versions of the legend, the word EMET, which means truth, is inscribed on the forehead of the golem. The golem grows. He becomes so tall that his master cannot reach him. He asks him to tie his shoes. The golem bends over, and the rabbi erases the aleph or first letter of EMET. This leaves MET—death. The golem turns to dust.

In another legend a rabbi or some rabbis, some magicians, create a golem and send it to another teacher, who is capable of making his own but is beyond such vanities. The rabbi speaks to it, but the golem does not answer, because he has been denied the powers of speech and understanding. The rabbi sentences him, "You are an artifice of magicians; return to your dust." The golem is destroyed.

Finally, another legend told by Scholem. A group of disciples—a single man cannot study and understand the *Book of Creation*—manages to create a golem. He is born with a dagger in his hands, and he begs his creators to destroy him, because "if I live I may be worshiped as an idol." For Israel, as for Protestantism, idolatry is one of the greatest sins. They kill the golem.

I have mentioned a few legends, but I would like to return to the beginning, to the doctrine that seems to me so worthy of attention. In each one of us there is a particle of divinity. This world, evidently, cannot be the work of an all-powerful and just god, but it depends on us. This is the lesson the Kabbalah gives us—beyond being a curiosity studied by historians or grammarians. Like the great poem of Hugo, *"Ce que dit la bouche d'ombre,"* the Kabbalah teaches the doctrine that the Greeks called *apokatastasis*: that all creatures, including Cain and the Devil, will return, at the end of great transmigrations, to be mingled again with the Divinity from which they once emerged.

❧ Blindness ❧

IN THE COURSE of the many lectures—too many lectures—I have given, I've observed that people tend to prefer the personal to the general, the concrete to the abstract. I will begin, then, by referring to my own modest blindness. Modest, because it is total blindness in one eye, but only partial in the other. I can still make out certain colors; I can still see blue and green. And yellow, in particular, has remained faithful to me. I remember when I was young I used to linger in front of certain cages in the Palermo zoo: the cages of the tigers and leopards. I lingered before the tigers' gold and black. Yellow is still with me, even now. I have written a poem entitled "The Gold of the Tigers," in which I refer to this friendship.

People generally imagine the blind as enclosed in a black world. There is, for example, Shakespeare's line: "Looking on darkness which the blind do see." If we understand *darkness* as *blackness*, then Shakespeare is wrong.

One of the colors that the blind—or at least this blind man—do *not* see is black; another is red. *Le rouge et le noir* are the colors denied us. I, who was accustomed to sleeping in total darkness, was bothered for a long time at having to sleep in this world of mist, in the greenish or bluish mist, vaguely luminous, which is the world of the blind. I wanted to lie down in darkness. The world of the blind is not the night that people imagine. (I should say that I am speaking for myself, and for my father and my grandmother, who both died blind—blind, laughing, and brave, as I also hope to die. They inherited many things—blindness, for example—but one does not inherit courage. I know that they were brave.)

The blind live in a world that is inconvenient, an undefined world from which certain colors emerge: for me, yellow, blue (except that the blue may be green), and green (except that the green may be blue). White has disappeared, or is confused with gray. As for red, it has vanished completely. But I hope some day—I am following a treatment— to improve and to be able to see that great color, that color which shines in poetry, and which has so many beautiful names in many languages. Think of *scharlach* in German, *scarlet* in English, *escarlata* in Spanish, *écarlate* in French. Words that are worthy of that great color. In contrast, *amarillo*, yellow, sounds weak in Spanish, in English it seems more like yellow. I think that in Old Spanish it was *amariello*.

I live in that world of colors, and if I speak of my own modest blindness, I do so, first, because it is not that perfect blindness which people imagine, and second, because it deals with me. My case is not especially dramatic. What is dramatic are those who suddenly lose their sight. In my case, that slow nightfall, that slow loss of sight, began when I began to see. It has continued since 1899 without dramatic moments, a slow nightfall that has lasted more than three quarters of a century. In 1955 the pathetic moment came when I knew I had lost my sight, my reader's and writer's sight.

In my life I have received many unmerited honors, but there is one which has made me happier than all the others: the directorship of the National Library. For reasons more political than literary, I was appointed by the Aramburu government.

I was named director of the library, and I returned to that building of which I had so many memories, on the Calle México in Monserrat, in the South of the city. I had never dreamed of the possibility of being director of the library. I had memories of another kind. I would go there with my father, at night. My father, a professor of psychology, would ask for some book by Bergson or William James, who were his favorite writers, or perhaps by Gustav Spiller. I, too timid to ask for a book, would look through some volume of the *Encyclopedia Britannica* or the German encyclopedias of Brockhaus or of Meyer. I would take a volume at random from the shelf and read. I remember one night when I was particularly rewarded, for I read three articles: on the Druids, the Druses, and Dryden—a gift of the letters *dr*. Other nights I was less fortunate.

I knew that Paul Groussac was in the building. I could have met him personally, but I was then quite shy; almost as shy as I am now. At the time, I believed that shyness was very important, but now I know that shyness is one of the evils one must try to overcome, that in reality to be shy doesn't matter—it is like so many other things to which one gives an exaggerated importance.

I received the nomination at the end of 1955. I was in charge of, I was told, a million books. Later I found out it was nine hundred thousand—a number that's more than enough. (And perhaps nine hundred thousand seems more than a million.)

Little by little I came to realize the strange irony of events. I had always imagined Paradise as a kind of library. Others think of a garden or of a palace. There I was, the center, in a way, of nine hundred thousand books in various languages, but I found I could barely make out the title pages and the spines. I wrote the "Poem of the Gifts," which begins:

> *No one should read self-pity or reproach*
> *into this statement of the majesty*
> *of God; who with such splendid irony*
> *granted me books and blindness at one touch.*
> [tr. Alastair Reid]

Those two gifts contradicted each other: the countless books and the night, the inability to read them.

I imagined the author of that poem to be Groussac, for Groussac was also the director of the library and also blind. Groussac was more courageous than I: he kept his silence. But I knew that there had certainly been moments when our lives had coincided, since we both had become blind and we both loved books. He honored literature with books far superior to mine. But we were both men of letters, and we both passed through the library of forbidden books— one might say, for our darkened eyes, of blank books, books without letters. I wrote of the irony of God, and in the end I asked myself which of us had written that poem of a plural I and a single shadow.

At the time I ignored the fact that there had been another director of the library who was blind, José Mármol. Here appears the number three, which seals everything. Two is a mere coincidence; three a confirmation. A con-

firmation of a ternary order, a divine or theological confirmation.

Mármol was director of the library when it was on the
Calle Venezuela. These days it is usual to speak badly of
Mármol, or not to mention him at all. But we must remember that when we speak of the time of Rosas, we do
not think of the admirable book by Ramos Mejía, *Rosas y
su tiempo* (*"Rosas and his time"*), but of the era as it is
described in Mármol's wonderfully gossipy novel, *La Amalia*.
To bequeath the image of an age or of a country is no small
glory.

We have, then, three people who shared the same fate.
And, for me, the joy of returning to the Monserrat section,
in the South. For everyone in Buenos Aires, the South is, in a
mysterious way, the secret center of the city. Not the other,
somewhat ostentatious center we show to tourists—in those
days there was not that bit of public relations called the
Barrio de San Telmo. But the South has come to be the
modest secret center of Buenos Aires.

When I think of Buenos Aires, I think of the Buenos
Aires I knew as a child: the low houses, the patios, the
porches, the cisterns with turtles in them, the grated win-
dows. That Buenos Aires was all of Buenos Aires. Now only
the southern section has been preserved. I felt that I had
returned to the neighborhood of my elders.

There were the books, but I had to ask my friends the
names of them. I remembered a sentence from Rudolf
Steiner, in his books on anthroposophy, which was the
name he gave to his theosophy. He said that when something
ends, we must think that something begins. His advice is
salutory, but the execution is difficult, for we only know
what we have lost, not what we will gain. We have a very

precise image—an image at times shameless—of what we have lost, but we are ignorant of what may follow or replace it.

I made a decision. I said to myself: since I have lost the beloved world of appearances, I must create something else. At the time I was a professor of English at the university. What could I do to teach that almost infinite literature, that literature which exceeds the life of a man, and even generations of men? What could I do in four Argentine months of national holidays and strikes? I did what I could to teach the love of that literature, and I refrained as much as possible from dates and names.

Some female students came to see me. They had taken the exam and passed. (All students pass with me!) To the girls—there were nine or ten—I said: "I have an idea. Now that you have passed and I have fulfilled my obligation as a professor, wouldn't it be interesting to embark on the study of a language or a literature we hardly know?" They asked which language and which literature. "Well, naturally the English language and English literature. Let us begin to study them, now that we are free from the frivolity of the exams; let us begin at the beginning."

I remembered that at home there were two books I could retrieve. I had placed them on the highest shelf, thinking I would never use them. They were Sweet's *Anglo-Saxon Reader* and *The Anglo-Saxon Chronicle*. Both had glossaries. And so we gathered one morning in the National Library.

I thought: I have lost the visible world, but now I am going to recover another, the world of my distant ancestors, those tribes of men who rowed across the stormy northern seas, from Germany, Denmark, and the Low Countries, who conquered England, and after whom we name England

—since *Angle-land*, land of the Angles, had previously been called the land of the Britons, who were Celts.

It was a Saturday morning. We gathered in Groussac's office, and we began to read. It was a situation that pleased and mortified us, and at the same time filled us with a certain pride. It was the fact that the Saxons, like the Scandinavians, used two runic letters to signify the two sounds of *th*, as in *thing* and *the*. This conferred an air of mystery to the page.

We were encountering a language which seemed different from English but similar to German. What always happens, when one studies a language, happened. Each one of the words stood out as though it had been carved, as though it were a talisman. For that reason the poems of a foreign language have a prestige they do not enjoy in their own language, for one hears, one sees, each one of the words individually. We think of the beauty, of the power, or simply of the strangeness of them.

We had good luck that morning. We discovered the sentence, "Julius Caesar was the first Roman to discover England." Finding ourselves with the Romans in a text of the North, we were moved. You must remember we knew nothing of the language; each word was a kind of talisman we unearthed. We found two words. And with those two words we became almost drunk. (It's true that I was an old man and they were young women—likely stages for inebriation.) I thought: "I am returning to the language my ancestors spoke fifty generations ago; I am returning to that language; I am reclaiming it. It is not the first time I speak it; when I had other names this was the language I spoke." Those two words were the name of London, *Lundenburh*, and the name of Rome, which moved us even more, thinking of the light that had fallen on those northern islands, *Romeburh*. I think we left crying, "*Lundenburh, Romeburh* . . ." in the streets.

Thus I began my study of Anglo-Saxon, which blindness brought me. And now I have a memory full of poetry that is elegiac, epic, Anglo-Saxon.

I had replaced the visible world with the aural world of the Anglo-Saxon language. Later I moved on to the richer world of Scandinavian literature: I went on to the Eddas and the sagas. I wrote *Ancient Germanic Literature* and many poems based on those themes, but most of all I enjoyed it. I am now preparing a book on Scandinavian literature.

I did not allow blindness to intimidate me. And besides, my editor made me an excellent offer: he told me that if I produced thirty poems in a year, he would publish a book. Thirty poems means discipline, especially when one must dictate every line, but at the same time it allows for a sufficient freedom, as it is impossible that in one year there will not be thirty occasions for poetry. Blindness has not been for me a total misfortune; it should not be seen in a pathetic way. It should be seen as a way of life: one of the styles of living.

Being blind has its advantages. I owe to the darkness some gifts: the gift of Anglo-Saxon, my limited knowledge of Icelandic, the joy of so many lines of poetry, of so many poems, and of having written another book, entitled, with a certain falsehood, with a certain arrogance, *In Praise of Darkness.*

I would like to speak now of other cases, of illustrious cases. I will begin with that obvious example of the friendship of poetry and blindness, with the one who has been called the greatest of poets: Homer. (We know of another blind Greek poet, Tamiris, whose work has been lost.

Tamiris was defeated in a battle with the muses, who broke his lyre and took away his sight.)

Oscar Wilde had a curious hypothesis, one which I don't think is historically correct but which is intellectually agreeable. In general, writers try to make what they say seem profound; Wilde was a profound man who tried to seem frivolous. He wanted us to think of him as a conversationalist; he wanted us to consider him as Plato considered poetry, as "that winged, fickle, sacred thing." Well, that winged, fickle, sacred thing called Oscar Wilde said that Antiquity had deliberately represented Homer as blind.

We do not know if Homer existed. The fact that seven cities vie for his name is enough to make us doubt his historicity. Perhaps there was no single Homer; perhaps there were many Greeks whom we conceal under the name of Homer. The traditions are unanimous in showing us a blind poet, yet Homer's poetry is visual, often splendidly visual—as was, to a far lesser degree, that of Oscar Wilde.

Wilde realized that his poetry was too visual, and he wanted to cure himself of that defect. He wanted to make poetry that was aural, musical—let us say like the poetry of Tennyson, or of Verlaine, whom he loved and admired so. Wilde said that the Greeks claimed that Homer was blind in order to emphasize that poetry must be aural, not visual. From that comes the *"de la musique avant toute chose"* of Verlaine and the symbolism contemporary to Wilde.

We may believe that Homer never existed, but that the Greeks imagined him as blind in order to insist on the fact that poetry is, above all, music; that poetry is, above all, the lyre; that the visual can or cannot exist in a poet. I know of great visual poets and great poets who are not visual—intellectual poets, mental ones—there's no need to mention names.

Let us go on to the example of Milton. Milton's blindness was voluntary. He knew from the beginning that he was going to be a great poet. This has occurred to other poets: Coleridge and De Quincey, before they wrote a single line, knew that their destiny was literary. I too, if I may mention myself, have always known that my destiny was, above all, a literary destiny—that bad things and some good things would happen to me, but that, in the long run, all of it would be converted into words. Particularly the bad things, since happiness does not need to be transformed: happiness is its own end.

Let us return to Milton. He destroyed his sight writing pamphlets in support of the execution of the king by Parliament. Milton said that he lost his sight voluntarily, defending freedom; he spoke of that noble task and never complained of being blind. He sacrificed his sight, and then he remembered his first desire, that of being a poet. They have discovered at Cambridge University a manuscript in which the young Milton proposes various subjects for a long poem.

"I might perhaps leave something so written to aftertimes, as they should not willingly let it die," he declared. He listed some ten or fifteen subjects, not knowing that one of them would prove prophetic: the subject of Samson. He did not know that his fate would, in a way, be that of Samson; that Samson, who had prophesied Christ in the Old Testament, also prophesied Milton, and with greater accuracy. Once he knew himself to be permanently blind, he embarked on two historical works, *A Brief History of Muscovia* and *A History of England*, both of which remained unfinished. And then the long poem *Paradise Lost*. He sought a theme that would interest all men, not merely the English. That subject was Adam, our common father.

He spent a good part of his time alone, composing verses, and his memory had grown. He would hold forty or fifty hendecasyllables of blank verse in his memory and then dictate them to whomever came to visit. The whole poem was written in this way. He thought of the fate of Samson, so close to his own, for now Cromwell was dead and the hour of the Restoration had come. Milton was persecuted and could have been condemned to death for having supported the execution of the king. But when they brought Charles II—son of Charles I, "The Executed"—the list of those condemned to death, he put down his pen and said, not without nobility, "There is something in my right hand which will not allow me to sign a sentence of death." Milton was saved, and many others with him.

He then wrote *Samson Agonistes*. He wanted to create a Greek tragedy. The action takes place in a single day, Samson's last. Milton thought on the similarity of destinies, since he, like Samson, had been a strong man who was ultimately defeated. He was blind. And he wrote those verses which, according to Landor, he punctuated badly, but which in fact had to be "Eyeless, in Gaza, at the mill, with the slaves"—as if the misfortunes were accumulating on Samson.

Milton has a sonnet in which he speaks of his blindness. There is a line one can tell was written by a blind man. When he has to describe the world, he says, "In this dark world and wide." It is precisely the world of the blind when they are alone, walking with hands outstretched, searching for props. Here we have an example—much more important than mine—of a man who overcomes blindness and does his work: *Paradise Lost*, *Paradise Regained*, *Samson Agonistes*, his best sonnets, part of *A History of the England*, from the beginnings to the Norman Conquest. All of this was executed while he was blind, all of it had to be dictated to casual visitors.

The Boston aristocrat Prescott was helped by his wife.

An accident, when he was a student at Harvard, had caused him to lose one eye and left him almost blind in the other. He decided that his life would be dedicated to literature. He studied, and learned, the literatures of England, France, Italy, and Spain. Imperial Spain offered him a world which was agreeable to his own rigid rejection of a democratic age. From an erudite he became a writer, and he dictated to his wife, who read to him, the histories of the conquest of Mexico and Peru, of the reign of the Catholic Kings and of Phillip II. It was a happy labor, almost impeccable, which took more than twenty years.

There are two examples which are closer to us. One I have already mentioned, Paul Groussac, who has been unjustly forgotten. People see him now as a French interloper in Argentina. It is said that his historical work has become dated, that today one makes use of greater documentation. But they forget that Groussac, like every writer, left two works: first, his subject, and second, the manner of its execution. Groussac revitalized Spanish prose. Alfonso Reyes, the greatest prose writer in Spanish in any era, once told me, "Groussac taught me how Spanish should be written." Groussac overcame his blindness and left some of the best pages in prose that have been written in our country. It will always please me to remember this.

Let us recall another example, one more famous than Groussac. In James Joyce we are also given a twofold work. We have those two vast and—why not say it?—unreadable novels, *Ulysses* and *Finnegans Wake*. But that is only half of his work (which also includes beautiful poems and the admirable *Portrait of an Artist as a Young Man*). The other half, and perhaps the most redeeming aspect (as they now say) is the fact that he took on the almost infinite English language. That language—which is statistically larger than all the others and offers so many possibilities for the writer, particularly in its concrete verbs—was not enough for him. Joyce, an Irishman, recalled that Dublin had been founded by Danish Vikings. He studied Norwegian—he wrote a letter to Ibsen in Norwegian—and then he studied Greek, Latin . . . He knew all the languages, and he wrote in a language invented by himself, difficult to understand but marked by a strange music. Joyce brought a new music to English. And he said, valorously (and mendaciously) that "of all the things that have happened to me, I think the least important was having been blind." Part of his vast work was executed in darkness: polishing the sentences in his memory, working at times for a whole day on a single phrase, and then writing it and correcting it. All in the midst of blindness or periods of blindness. In comparison, the impotence of Boileau, Swift, Kant, Ruskin, and George Moore was a melancholic instrument for the successful execution of their work; one might say the same of perversion, whose beneficiaries today have ensured that no one will ignore their names. Democritus of Abdera tore his eyes out in a garden so that the spectacle of reality would not distract him; Origen castrated himself.

I have enumerated enough examples. Some are so illustrious that I am ashamed to have spoken of my own personal case—except for the fact that people always hope for confessions and I have no reason to deny them mine. But, of course, it seems absurd to place my name next to those I have recalled.

I have said that blindness is a way of life, a way of life that is not entirely unfortunate. Let us recall those lines of the greatest Spanish poet, Fray Luis de León:

> *Vivir quiero conmigo,*
> *gozar quiero del bien que debo al cielo,*
> *a solas sin testigo,*

> *libre de amor, de celo,*
> *de odio, de esperanza, de recelo.*

[I want to live with myself,| I want to enjoy
the good that I owe to heaven,| alone, without
witnesses,| free of love, of jealousy,| of hate, of
hope, of fear.]

Edgar Allen Poe knew this stanza by heart.

For me, to live without hate is easy, for I have never felt hate. To live without love I think is impossible, happily impossible for each one of us. But the first part— "I want to live with myself,/ I want to enjoy the good that I owe to heaven"—if we accept that in the good of heaven there can also be darkness, then who lives more with themselves? Who can explore themselves more? Who can know more of themselves? According to the Socratic phrase, who can know himself more than the blind man?

A writer lives. The task of being a poet is not completed at a fixed schedule. No one is a poet from eight to twelve and from two to six. Whoever is a poet is one always, and continually assaulted by poetry. I suppose a painter feels that colors and shapes are besieging him. Or a musician feels that the strange world of sounds—the strangest world of art—is always seeking him out, that there are melodies and dissonances looking for him. For the task of an artist, blindness is not a total misfortune. It may be an instrument. Fray Luis de León dedicated one of his most beautiful odes to Francisco Salinas, a blind musician.

A writer, or any man, must believe that whatever happens to him is an instrument; everything has been given for an end. This is even stronger in the case of the artist. Everything that happens, including humiliations, embarrassments, misfortunes, all has been given like clay, like material for one's art. One must accept it. For this reason I speak in a poem of the ancient food of heroes: humiliation, unhappiness, discord. Those things are given to us to transform, so that we may make from the miserable circumstances of our lives things that are eternal, or aspire to be so.

If a blind man thinks this way, he is saved. Blindness is a gift. I have exhausted you with the gifts it has given me. It gave me Anglo-Saxon, it gave me some Scandinavian, it gave me a knowledge of a Medieval literature I had ignored, it gave me the writing of various books, good or bad, but which justified the moment in which they were written. Moreover, blindness has made me feel surrounded by the kindness of others. People always feel good will toward the blind.

I want to end with a line of Goethe: *"Alles Nahe werde fern,"* everything near becomes distant. Goethe was referring to the evening twilight. Everything near becomes distant. It is true. At nightfall, the things closest to us seem to move away from our eyes. So the visible world has moved away from my eyes, perhaps forever.

Goethe could be referring not only to twilight but to life. All things go off, leaving us. Old age is probably the supreme solitude—except that the supreme solitude is death. And "everything near becomes distant" also refers to the slow process of blindness, of which I hoped to show, speaking tonight, that it is not a complete misfortune. It is one more instrument among the many—all of them so strange—that fate or chance provide.